Peace Within, Peace Between:

Your Relationship Toolkit

Peace Within, Peace Between:

Your Relationship Toolkit

Linda Powers Leviton, M.A.

Science & Behavior Books, Inc.
Palo Alto, California 94306 USA
www.sbbks.com

Published by Science & Behavior Books, Inc.
Palo Alto, CA. www.sbbks.com

Copyright ©2014 by Linda Powers Leviton
All rights reserved.
No part of this book may be reproduced
without permission from the author.

Printed in the United States of America

ISBN-13: 978-0-9911236-8-1

ISBN-10: 0991123689

LLCN: 2013922404

Cover Design by
Chip Borkenhagen/RiverPlace Communication Arts
Interior Design by
Larry Seward, Granada Hills, CA
Interior Art by
Linda Powers Leviton, Granada Hills, CA

Dedication

In Loving Memory of My Father,

Ben Powers
(1925-2012)

&

**To my wonderful children,
Michael, Josh, and Miriam**

*There are no words to describe
the depth of my love for
these three wonderful young adults*

Table of Contents

Foreword i

Acknowledgments iii

Introduction v

Part One: Bugs with Solutions 1

    Chapter One: Beginnings 3

        Worksheet for Chapter One: Beginnings 15

    Chapter Two: Helpers 17

        Worksheet for Chapter 2: Resources 29

Part Two: New Information 31

    Chapter Three: Connection 33

        Worksheet for Chapter 3: Connection 43

    Chapter Four: Contact 45

        Worksheet for Chapter 4: Contact 55

    Chapter Five: Growth 57

        Worksheet for Chapter 5: Growth 67

    Chapter Six: Intimacy 69

        Worksheet for Chapter 6: Intimacy 79

Part Three: Getting To Know Your Self 81

    Chapter Seven: Learning Styles 83

        Worksheet for Chapter 7: Learning Styles 93

    Chapter Eight: Personality 95

        Worksheet for Chapter 8: Personality 107

    Chapter Nine: Core Values 109

        Worksheet for Chapter Nine: Core Values 121

  Chapter Ten: Assessment **123**

    Worksheet for Chapter Ten: Assessment 131

Part Four: Old Business, New Possibilities **133**

  Chapter Eleven: Past, Present, and Future **135**

    Worksheet for Chapter Eleven: Past, Present, and Future 141

  Chapter Twelve: Parents and Others **143**

    Worksheet for Chapter 12: Parents and Others 155

  Chapter Thirteen: Communication **159**

    Worksheet for Chapter 13: Communication 171

  Chapter Fourteen: The Tip of the Iceberg **175**

    Worksheet for Chapter 14: Behavior, Coping Stances & Defenses 189

  Chapter Fifteen: Conclusion, Hopes & Wishes **193**

References/Bibliography **197**

Index **201**

Foreword

by **Linda Kreger Silverman Ph.D.**

Virginia Satir's profound wisdom is the inspiration and foundation of this beautiful book. Linda Leviton has artfully captured Satir's philosophy and her therapeutic strategies, introducing Satir to new audiences. *Peace Within, Peace Between* serves the Satir community by illustrating her principles with stories and art. It serves those who are new to Satir's Family Therapy by making these principles and practices easily accessible to both therapists and those who seek personal growth.

Parents will find *Peace Within, Peace Between* an enlightening guide to creating harmonious family relationships. In the spirit of Satir, every family member is treated with respect. Linda has decades of experience helping families overcome obstacles and develop new modes of communication. As a parent herself, she has faced many of the same demons. For many years, her family has participated in Satir Family Camp, where they forged strong, loving bonds.

Individuals seeking to improve their relationships will discover in reading *Peace Within, Peace Between* that the first step is self-appreciation. Each chapter contains exercises to assist readers in understanding their learning styles, their personality styles, their triumphs, their inner resources, their core values, their role models, and their capacity for growth. This essential inner work enables the person to appreciate others and to create positive connections with others.

Therapists will find Linda Leviton's applications of Satir's model a welcome addition to their work, regardless of their philosophical orientation. The book contains dozens of practical ideas for self-help and helping others. Interwoven throughout *Peace Within, Peace Between* are stories of breakdowns in communication and how they were resolved. Readers will learn ways of communicating more effectively with individuals who have learning and personality styles different from their own.

The message on every page is that change is not only possible—it is inevitable. The cycle of change from crisis to chaos to the integration of new possibilities is never ending. *Peace Within, Peace Between* is a manual for directing the process of change in a positive manner that is respectful of everyone involved.

A word about giftedness is in order. Linda and I have worked together for 5 decades to help the plight of misunderstood gifted children and adults. Contrary to public opinion, the gifted are not always "successful." More often than not they are outsiders in society who have a difficult time fitting in. And even if they succeed at becoming what others want them to be, they experience the hollow emptiness of having given up their real selves in the bargain. Virginia Satir was a gifted woman. And those who have had the depth of mind and heart to follow her work are, by and large, an exceptional group.

Many of the anecdotes in this book are based on Linda's work with gifted families. These families deal with many of the same issues as other families, albeit with heightened intensity and complexity. They also deal with issues that are unique to this population. All atypical groups that are marginalized by society because of their differences face a unique set of challenges. Creative individuals will delight in Linda's original artwork and her creative suggestions for solving problems. Creativity is giftedness.

My life has been personally enriched by Linda Leviton's presence in it. I delight in her generosity of spirit, her ability to love others unconditionally, her endless creativity, her willingness to reveal her vulnerability, her talent as a therapist, and her authenticity. May *Peace Within, Peace Between* bring hope to all who enter these pages.

Linda Silverman

Acknowledgments and Appreciations

I never met Virginia Satir; yet I am profoundly grateful for the legacy she created through books, tapes, presentations, trainings, and the organizations she founded: Satir Global Network, formerly Avanta (a professional training organization for friends and colleagues); The Beautiful People (later renamed IHLRN—International Human Learning Resource Network); and Satir Family Camp. My friends and colleagues in these organizations continue to promote Satir's vision "Peace within, peace between, and peace among" all over the world.

Many other mentors have contributed to my life and ability to write this book. In particular I lovingly acknowledge*:*

-Dr. Linda Silverman, my dearest friend and lifelong mentor, who has provided encouragement and support at every stage of my life in all possible ways—I am forever indebted to her for her wisdom, nurturance, counsel, time, encouragement, editorial contributions, love and endless belief in my contribution to the world. This book would not have seen the light of day without her efforts.

-Nancy Macdonald, Virginia Satir's friend and my writing muse; she generously shared her resources, knowledge, experience and time to support this project in its infancy. She read and commented on several versions of the first draft, and encouraged me at every stage of its creation.

I would also like to thank:

- Bob and Becky Spitzer, my publisher and dear friends, who encouraged me from the beginning and made publication a reality.

- My family for providing the love, support, and the valuable lessons I needed to learn.

- My beloved and supportive friends and colleagues from all over the United States and Canada who blessed me over the decades in countless ways—my girlfriends, my goddess circle, my book groups, my mariposas, my women's groups, and the all who have appreciated and supported me over the years. Thank-yous to Steve Gomes, for the initial facilitation of the project, Ron Nelson who held my hand through the final year of gestation, Elizabeth

Seward who helped with final edits, and Larry Seward, who spent months helping me edit, format, and craft the final version of the book.

- And last but not least, I appreciate all my clients; those who proved my love-filled message was valuable, and especially those who encouraged me to share their stories and successes.

Introduction

"I want you to get excited about who you are, what you are, what you have, and what can still be for you. I want to inspire you to see that you can go far beyond where you are right now."
— Virginia Satir

I've written this book to provide the practical knowledge, concrete skills, and behavioral practices necessary to create the life your heart yearns to live. While we each have unique individual goals and longings, most of us also yearn for lives of purpose, passion and mutually fulfilling relationships. We want to feel that we have contributed something valuable to the world. Based on the models and wisdom of family therapy founder Virginia Satir, the ideas in this book offer the possibility of creating a more satisfying life by achieving peace within yourself, and in all your relationships.

Satir's hallmark quote "Peace within, peace between, peace among" is both the goal of her work, and the blessing she lovingly bestowed on us. This year, 2013, marks the 25th anniversary of her death; yet the organizations she founded, the theories she taught and the legacy she built continue. I selected *Peace Within, Peace Between* as the title of this book for several reasons: first as a homage to Satir for her models and insights, which form the backbone of the book; secondly to indicate that the goal of the book is to provide a map to achieving a peaceful relationship with yourself so you can craft harmonious relationships with others. I left out the last phrase, "Peace among" because this refers to a more global sense of peace. I believe that this can result from applying the skills and love-based practices I describe; however, this book is meant to help you create the life **you** desire.

Peace Within, Peace Between is loosely structured in the format of Virginia Satir's meeting model, The Temperature Reading:

- *Acknowledgments* expresses appreciation for all those who have contributed to the process of creating this book.
- *Part One: Bugs with Solutions* defines resources that can facilitate positive solutions.
- *Part Two: New Information* explains what concepts are fundamental to achieving personal and interpersonal goals.
- *Part Three: Getting to Know Yourself* explores the unique personal traits that both define and challenge us.
- *Part Four: Old Business/ New Possibilities* maps the journey and describes some destinations.

- *Conclusion - Hopes and Wishes* surveys the book's messages and expresses my hopes and wishes for you going forward to apply all the above.

Being sensitive to learning style differences (detailed in Chapter Seven: Learning Styles), I've written this book with elements that make it more accessible to everyone. As a visual-spatial learner, I personally gravitate toward anecdotes, metaphors and illustrations to absorb concepts. For the auditory-sequential learners, I've explained each concept as concisely and linearly as possible in the body of the text. For tactile-kinesthetic learners, I've provided bullet points and worksheets that allow them to apply the concepts. Additionally, it is not necessary to start at the beginning and read to the end to profit from these ideas. In fact, there is no "best" way to absorb this material. I encourage you to approach this information in whichever way appeals to *you*.

This journey, as all of life, includes many opportunities to adapt and change both behaviors and presuppositions. Every new concept or action assimilated, large or small, has the potential to positively influence the future. Life is a kaleidoscope of experience and choice that culminates in a unique story, vibrantly peppered with both challenges and blessings. Each of us has the potential to live in many dimensions at once: the present—a fleeting heartbeat bookmarked by future and past; the past—filled with what has already happened, illuminated by the wisdom gleaned from those experiences; the future—a page yet to be filled, ripe with possibility. We have so many choices about how to create just one out of infinite possible futures. This book is about learning from the past, living the present, and providing options for a beautiful future.

I could not be a psychotherapist if I didn't believe that change is always possible, and that we are all capable of surviving and learning something from every challenge. Applying the techniques and models in this book—not to mention the support of lots of wonderful friends, mentors and coaches—I have survived and grown stronger through a lifetime of challenges and losses. These techniques work in part because they are practical and they address our deepest hope that we have the power to improve our circumstances.

The focus of this book and this work is on the *possibility* in each of us—the potential to use our inner strength, wisdom, beauty, and innate goodness to create the life we yearn to live. Virginia Satir facilitated thousands of transformations for families and individuals, regardless of age, race, culture or geography. She loved people exactly as we all are: a work in progress, capable of anything and everything.

In traditional psychotherapy, the focus is the past, understanding today's complaints as caused by something or someone from the past. There is a belief that being conscious of the "problem" and its source will be enough to banish it from the future. It is one way of conceptualizing a problem. But it didn't explain why we kept repeating patterns, even after we'd gained insight into their source. It felt like a condemnation of the resources that helped mold us, instead of the celebration of survival and growth that they represent. Virginia Satir's theories and models appealed to me, because they are practical applications of what we can learn from our life experience: "The past happened. What did we learn from it? Great, now what do we want to do with that? Let's be grateful for that opportunity (and that is it past) and now add a new idea, a new skill and *apply it if it fits and we choose to do so!*" No victims—only anthropologists, detectives, and playwrights.

Virginia Satir gave us hope by treating us with respect and believing in us. Her models provided the vehicle to navigate the road ahead. In providing the healing idea that our parents did the best they could—even though they were human and made mistakes—we could finally feel their love and appreciate their good intentions. Giving ourselves compassion, wisdom, and a new perception of our past helps us craft a better future, without the previous regret, guilt, blame, and hurt that stayed with us when we carried an open wound.

This belief, that we could create a better future, is what drives all of Satir's models. "If we know we want to have better relationships with ourselves and others, we can make that happen, and here's how," she purred in a seductive, trance-producing way. My voice has been one that echoes Satir's belief that "anything is possible."

Much of my work has been with the community of people labeled gifted and creative. In reality, we all have gifts and we all are creators of our own lives. Our thoughts, behaviors, and hopes create our futures. Those with a gifted label may have a different, faster, more complex, or more colorful way of living, but it is important to remember that our emotional life is commensurately more complicated and intense as well. It is not better or worse; but it is intensely painful and confusing at times.

Additionally, parts of this book include ideas and models that are not found within the Satir framework. I have included these because I feel that knowledge is the first step towards understanding. Because we only see the world through our own eyes, we are at risk of condemning anything different. If we understand the "other," we are better able to accommodate and appreciate them.

My goal in writing this book has been to inspire hope, encourage action, and provide options—concrete tools and ideas for creating the relationships and future interactions needed to fulfill our yearning to be loved and appreciated for our authentic, unique, beautiful selves.

Often, we are our own worst critics. We can't forgive our own frailty, our own humanity, let alone that of the people who nurtured us as best they could. My hope is that we all learn to forgive each other for our human flaws and appreciate our loving intentions and shared yearnings. By practicing, teaching and modeling the positive, respect-filled communication and life strategies that Satir practiced, we all have a chance of healing ourselves, and the world.

The answers to all our questions lie within us. My hope is this book is the key that unlocks those answers that lie within you. I think you will be pleased with what you find within yourself, and how much happier that will make you in your life and the world.

In Judaism there is a concept that we each have our own responsibility of Tikkun Olam, healing the world. It is my hope that the wisdom contained in these pages will inspire your purpose and passion for living the life you choose, and also sharing your light in ways that will illuminate darkness in the world.

"Peace within, peace between, and peace among" — Virginia Satir

Linda Powers Leviton

Part One: Bugs with Solutions

"I can't light your light. I can only light mine so that I can illuminate for you to see to light your own light." — *Virginia Satir*

Peace Within, Peace Between

Chapter One: Beginnings

"The task of the therapist is to see the light that shines in every person or family, and to uncoil the wrappings that shroud that light."
— *Virginia Satir*

In the pages that follow we will explore Virginia Satir's change process through the application of her theories and models. These practical tools can be used by individuals to improve their own relationships, or by professionals to inspire growth in others. Apply those that fit in whatever order helps you create a life you love.

Six years after her death, Virginia Satir began to change my life. Satir, "the mother of family therapy," died in 1988. Since then, her colleagues and protégés have continued to teach her ideas and successfully introduce her interactive models all over the world. Her theories work whether applied to individuals, couples, or families, in schools or work settings, and regardless of economic, cultural, racial, or religious differences.

Not everything in this book is strictly Satir's work. The practices described here are based on a solid Satir foundation, but represent a synthesis of diverse ideas from many fine minds that have inspired creative solutions to a variety of challenges.

We are all experts about our own particular processes, motivations and learning styles. In addition to devoting a chapter to the three main learning styles, I've written this book in a way to appeal to all styles, complete with illustrations and exercises to help anchor each idea. Just as the chapters don't need to be read in a particular order, the exercises do not need to be completed sequentially.

When Satir worked with a family in front of an audience, she would often stop in the middle of the client's emotional explanation and ask the audience, "Does anyone else here know anything about this feeling?" As much of the audience raised their hands, shame evaporated and the client could move on to the next level of the transformation. I have included the stories of some of my clients to achieve a similar purpose. We are never alone in our feelings, even if we fear we might be. Many of the clients described in these stories have multiple challenges, or exceptionalities. Some have emotional, learning, or physical challenges. Some are cognitively advanced (gifted). All have one thing in common—they are in pain and wish for relief.

Part of the beauty of this work is that I speak as a therapist and from my heart. In my life, these two approaches are the same. In the spirit of being open…

I believe that:

- Everyone deserves to be treated with kindness, respect and integrity. (*We must earn respect, but human beings all deserve respectful treatment*).

- We know more about ourselves than anyone else does. (*We are always here*).

- We all start with the universal yearning to feel capable, productive, loved and lovable (*though some of us lose hope of that ever happening*).

- We all have challenges to overcome, ways we can improve and gifts to contribute (*so we can fulfill our highest and best purpose in life*).

- We all want to be able to act authentically and still be liked and accepted (*even when we fall short of expectations or goals*).

- All wisdom gleaned from life experience is necessary to become conscious and whole. (*Experiences always include lessons; it is our challenge to uncover the best one*).

- If we don't learn the lesson of our challenges, we will probably get another chance soon enough (*unfortunately*).

- Change is inevitable; how we deal with it can lead to countless different outcomes. (*Every choice can result in a new possibility*).

- Every outcome has value. (*Ultimately, we write the end of the story*).

- The therapeutic process should be tailored to meet each of our unique needs (*not to fit the therapist's orientation*).

- The therapeutic relationship may be one-sided, but it is nonetheless intimate and deeply impactful.

Note: Clients pay for my time, expertise, training and experience—the love is a gift…

With every client, my first goal is to address their yearnings in ways that open the door for fulfilling and lasting positive change—if they leave feeling lovable, they have the foundation necessary to accomplish everything else. One of my favorite aphorisms is, "Pain is inevitable, suffering optional." Many of the tools I use to help people avoid suffering are included in this book.

We all start life with an innate sense of trust. A baby cries hoping she will be heard and her needs met. Sometimes, if ignored long enough, she will die because those cries receive no response. Failure to Thrive Syndrome happens when the baby loses hope. Many adults suffer from a type of "Failure to Thrive." We all want to feel better, to be happy, and to connect more positively with people in our lives. Though it may seem that some people are evil or destructive, upon deeper inspection, we usually find all behavior happens for a reason. That reason is not always useful to achieve a current goal. When we understand what created and drives the behavior, we often can manifest an opportunity for a different future.

I have yet to meet a child I would consider evil, or a parent who desires to hurt his or her child for no reason. Satir maintained that parents are the best parents they know how to be at that moment. But both parents and children can feel distressed and powerless; their behavior will demonstrate those feelings. When I meet these families, I am always aware of the disappointment, hurt and fear that lurks beneath the anger and hopelessness. This compassion and empathy creates the possibility of transformative change.

The models and exercises that follow are designed to restore hope that better relationships and more effective communication are achievable. Each new positive experience proves the value of the effort.

Dealing with Change

Change is inevitable. People are born, marry, divorce, move, change jobs, get sick, heal; all these things remind us we are still among the living. As we face these new events, we experience some degree of disintegration of the "who and what" we were before those events affected us and threw us into a state of chaos. Satir created her Change Process model to help us tolerate and pass through that uncomfortable "chaos" phase. Below is an expanded version of that model that shows the developmental steps that occur and reoccur during the change process.

The Change Process

1) **Status Quo** (Familiar, knows exactly what to expect and to do)

2) **FOREIGN ELEMENT** (Something happens to upset the Status Quo)

3) **Crisis** begins—try to regain the Status Quo or WHAT?

4) **Chaos** (Unpleasant, confusing, painful, disorienting, upsetting, anxiety producing...will do anything to regain the comfort of the Status Quo)

5) *Dismemberment & Disorganization* (Falling apart? Coming or going?)

6) **?Choice Point? Re-entry or Regression?** (Seeing a light at the end of the tunnel vs. swimming upstream to regain the Old Status Quo)

7) **FINDING RESOURCES** (Friends, Family, Therapist, Spiritual Leader, Community)

8) **Building strength, courage & faith. Learning from mistakes**

9) *Mourning the past* (Hopes, what might have been)

10) *Finding empathy for yourself & others*

11) **Integrating the new possibilities**

12) **Practicing new ways of being & thinking**

13) **NEW STATUS QUO** (Eventually becomes the Status Quo again, and Cycle begins again)

This book is about creating small changes that heal and promote progress—in spite of our fears and resistance. In this context, the change process is one of co-creation and tapping into what we already know. Most of the time, we cling to the status quo not because it is ideal, or even better than the alternative; we resist change because of fear. The familiar is comfortable. But, when we make decisions out of fear (as of the unknown, or of a negative consequence) we rarely make the best choice.

Part of the process of transformation is being able to muster the patience to survive the inevitable challenges (Foreign Elements) and the subsequent discomfort (Crisis and Chaos) that life provides. Like it or not, life does not let us stay in the status quo for long. Even life cycle events, like birth, marriage, children leaving home, moving, or job loss can disrupt the status quo. We develop the resilience needed to grow when we accept and expect that Chaos must precede Reintegration.

"Not another growth opportunity," we whine. And yet, without them, we often would not choose to take the risks that allow progress and growth.

Steps to Embracing a New Possibility

1. Welcome the Foreign Element.
2. Embrace the Chaos as a time to regroup, a fresh start.
3. Look for the lesson to learn by seeing dismemberment as a chance to study the parts.
4. Feel gratitude for the help and care of the resources you find.
5. Integrate by rebuilding a better version.
6. Practice the new way of being with pride in your achievement.
7. Thank the Old Status Quo for its previous service.
8. Appreciate the New Status Quo for providing new opportunities.

Wholeness

When we feel safe, hopeful, competent, loved and lovable, we are more likely to ask for what we want and need. When we get what we need we are more likely to feel whole—to have resilience so we can weather life's problems, transitions, and challenges.

Many of us manage to get our basic life needs met without experiencing much joy in the process. We feel that we are missing something. We don't fully enjoy or participate in life. This can cause physical complaints, illness, emotional distress and, eventually, hopelessness. We find ways to cope with these discomforts; excessive eating, substance abuse, and sexual addictions are all symptoms that we don't feel complete or fulfilled. If we don't feel whole, we try to find something to fill the gaps. Often we expect another person to serve this purpose.

Relationships will rarely repair our feelings of inadequacy or fill the internal emptiness that plagues many of us. One of my favorite children's books is *The Missing Piece Meets the Big O* by Shel Silverstein. It is a fable about how becoming whole is preferable to trying to be or fill a missing piece.

Becoming Whole

The first step in the process of becoming whole is imagining what that would look like, and how the journey towards achieving it might begin. Everything ever created began as an idea.

If we step back and consider our past choices and behavior patterns the way a sociologist studies people, we can start to put together a picture of the various parts that constitute who we are. The worksheet for this chapter will help you create an image of your best self, and you can use that information to identify and imagine what you need to feel whole.

> **Questions for Your Inner Sociologist to Ponder**
> - How are your old behaviors different from your current ones?
> - Are you proud of your past or regretful?
> - What would you keep the same? Change?

In Search of "Wholeness"

Parts of our innate personality are in place at birth. Many of the traits that define us as unique are genetically inherited. Gunderson and Berkowitz's (2006) study of Borderline Personality Disorder found "levels of heritability" of "inborn biogenetic temperaments" (a predisposition to a disorder such as Bipolar Disorder) to be 68%. Laurence Wright (1998) studied twins, "Amy and Beth," who were adopted at birth into completely different family environments; he found they turned out "astoundingly similar" (especially in dysfunctional pathologies).

So we are born with much of our temperament, personality, and intelligence—the building blocks of being whole. Yet, the 20% or more of our personality that comes from our environment and experience makes a huge difference.

Before Timothy Leary became famous for his experiments with hallucinogenic drugs, he developed an extensive theory defining personality characteristics (Leary, 1957). He found that each characteristic could result in opposite extremes of outcome. The same personality trait, such as tenacity, could result in either a Mother Theresa or a Hitler, depending upon the environmental influences that shaped that trait. So, while Mother Theresa presumably had Jesus' teachings and behavior as a model, Hitler might have had someone who taught and practiced hate and destruction. All this underscores the importance of understanding all influences, whether they are inborn or environmental. Once we do this, we can begin to look at maximizing our potentials and possibilities.

Inventory Ideas

- Make a list of your personality traits.
- List how each trait might be used for your highest and best purpose.
- List how each trait could undermine reaching your highest and best purpose.
- What are your personality assets and liabilities?
- Are there any contexts in which your liabilities are assets or a vice?

Positive Change in the Service of Progress

It's easy to feel powerless in this day and age. As individuals, it is difficult to change the world, which has serious problems. Even the people closest to us may or may not have a tolerance for change. Individual need for change varies across a continuum—some people want to keep everything the same and will resist any change no matter how useful, while some of us love change and need to change things all the time; we embrace differences and search for ways to improve everything. In the center of the continuum are those who may like gradual change, or intermittent change. Neurolinguistic Programming (Bandler & Grinder, 1979) teaches us to tailor the words we use to the needs of the listener; high change people respond to words like "new" and "innovative," while their opposites respond better to words that minimize the change, or suggest a gradual consideration of it, like "consider…." or "think about the possibility…." But the greatest resistance to change comes from the fact that we are attracted to familiar situations.

> *For years, Tina was hurt and confused when her parents refused all her great ideas for solving the problems they described as intractable. Once she understood that she and her parents were at the opposite ends of the "change continuum," she began to understand that what inspired and invigorated her left her parents anxious and dismayed. Changing how she made suggestions, and understanding their internal resistance to change in general (not to her or her suggestions), allowed her to stop taking these rejections personally.*

Capacity for Change

Satir created her interactive models to demonstrate how powerful we are. Banning blame, she uncovered basic truths and human commonalities to demonstrate we have the power to change our reactions to our experience. She illuminated how we sabotage our labors and how we can start using more positive coping behaviors. She created models to help us "birth" a new way of being that will more effectively allow us to fulfill our yearnings and goals. I am sharing many of them with you.

Small changes in our behavior and perception can translate into big changes in our thoughts, feelings and reactions. This not only affects how others treat us and our relationships; it improves how we feel about ourselves.

> **Resources Under Our Control**
> - Our behaviors
> - Our prejudices and judgments
> - Our beliefs
> - The contexts we choose
> - Our choices
> - Many of our life situations
> - Our reactions to what happens
> - Our perceptions of what we see, hear and feel
> - How we treat ourselves and others
> - The meanings we make about what happens to us

A smiling person is rarely treated the same as a neutral or frowning person. Even when we are talking on the phone, people can "hear" a smile in our voice. In most cultures, a smile communicates good will, happiness, and positive intention—all characteristics more likely to initiate a positive connection. A smile can affect interactions in all kinds of unanticipated ways. What's more, a smile costs nothing, and is available to anyone at any time. There is a caveat, however. The energy behind the smile, the goodwill, is what creates the magical difference.

Kathy smiled all the time, including when someone was yelling at her and she really felt like crying, or when she was nervous. If in a group there was a lull in the conversation, there would be Kathy with a big grin on her face. It turned out that Kathy had a very punitive father who would beat her for crying or looking sad. "If you cry, I'll really give you something to cry about." Unconsciously, smiling was a way of protecting herself. Kathy was very sad inside so her smile did not communicate anything except pain and incongruence.

If we smile when we don't feel like smiling, it is likely to block the positive energy that a smile is meant to convey. This is called being incongruent—when how we feel, and how we look or act don't match. I'll explain more about the power of congruence in later chapters. Consider this a peek at our most powerful communication and inner health goal. Being consistently congruent, and feeling whole, will make you authentically want to smile.

Obstacles

In the course of growing up, we learn that some of our characteristics are not acceptable to some of our loved ones. The process of selecting what we are going to change or hide about our true Self can be positive. Let's use violence as an example. Most people agree that punching someone isn't the best way to resolve conflict—it can be unlawful and have devastating consequences. We learn other ways to control violent urges or better ways to express anger. We aren't surprised if we get arrested for hitting another adult. Yet, in certain circumstances, even violence is tolerated (such as hitting your child for breaking a rule) or in war (when your country might force you to kill an enemy). These exceptions and gray areas can stop us from being fully congruent, and we cannot feel whole without it.

Additionally, some behaviors might only bother a particular person, such as when a father believes his son should never cry. When we are forced to curb our authentic needs, we make a meaning about whether we, or our feelings, are acceptable. Because we want to believe that our parents love us, we tend to internalize their disapproval: "No one could love a boy who cries (otherwise, my father would still love me even if I cried), so I'm not lovable *because* I cry" or maybe "Something is wrong with me because even my father (who must love me) can't accept me when I cry." In either case, the boy learns that either he must stop crying (become inauthentic) or he is unacceptable. Multiply this by the hundreds of behaviors that a particular parent may criticize and you have a child with lots of reasons to feel unacceptable.

> *A mother tells her child to play silently. She spanks him when he makes noise. He resents being punished for his authentic expression of joy or anger, but he concludes that his authentic self may not be acceptable because his mother ("who must love him") doesn't like that part of him. Mom may have a good reason for wanting the quiet, but the child has learned he cannot be authentic and get the approval he needs from Mom.*
>
> *Later, as the child goes into the world, he observes that other children aren't expected to be silent, and don't get punished for playing noisily. He then has to struggle with the understanding that only his own mother is unable to accept that part of his authentic self. At that moment, he must make a new meaning to incorporate this new information. Many meanings are possible: the other children are wrong or bad and their mothers just ignore it; his inauthentic behavior is superior and his mother has done him a favor to make him better than the other children; his mother is unfair or has reasons he can't know for wanting him to be quiet; or his mother doesn't love him as much as other mothers love their children.*

Each of those meanings will have a different effect upon a child and can change his or her sense of self, as well as his or her decisions about the future. Human beings are designed to make meaning and find patterns from their experience because understanding is reassuring, and confusion is uncomfortable. Unfortunately, not all the meanings we make are accurate; the implications of believing an inaccurate meaning can be catastrophic to the relationship.

This process of *experience/perception/meaning-making/feeling* happens throughout life. It shapes how we see ourselves and others. If we learn to feel shame and guilt around our normal impulses, we start to hide those parts of us that seem unacceptable. We might also inaccurately interpret what we see and hear—violence might actually be anger, disappointment, or fear. Other behaviors might have been stifled for unfair or quixotic reasons, but we believe they make us unacceptable. These are the feelings and beliefs that stand in the way of feeling whole and authentic.

Worksheet for Chapter One: Beginnings

Question: *Was there ever a time that you felt better about yourself than you do at this moment?*

Activity: *Make a list of times you felt better than you do now, and what exactly was different about it.*

Times I Felt Better	**What Was Different About it?**
Example:	
I could climb a flight of stairs without huffing and puffing when I was in college.	*I weighed my correct weight, I walked everywhere and got lots of exercise, I took vitamins, and the air was clean there.*
1.	
2.	
3.	
4.	
5.	

Challenge: *Select one of the above as something you'd like to work on now. Write a plan for beginning the change process*

Chapter Two: Helpers

"The people helper can only offer his or her resources, not demand they be accepted. Your job as a therapist is to help people use their experiences for growth, and to find a way to integrate all of their experiences."
— *Virginia Satir*

Finding Help

When we go to doctors, we describe our symptoms. They diagnose and treat us based on what they know about other people who have described those symptoms in the past. They may know more about disease, but they don't know more about us. They make a meaning based on what *we* tell them, and what they observe. Usually this is enough, but when we are unaware of the critical symptom and they cannot see anything wrong, they need more information—*from us*. In other words, we provide most of the information the doctor needs to help us. In spite of all this, many doctors act as if their contributions are more relevant than ours. Could they really diagnose, let alone cure, our problems without us and our bodies providing the information? In a hierarchical system, "experts" believe they know more about us than we do ourselves.

Unfortunately, most traditional therapy is also based on this hierarchical medical model. "Patients" are generally discouraged from participating in the strategic part of the therapeutic process. The clients are expected to blindly trust their therapists with virtually no idea what they believe, what core values they hold, what treatment they plan to use, what goals they have for therapy, or what they might have experienced in their personal life. Some therapists will even indignantly fire clients for trying to "control the treatment plan."

In Satir therapy, therapists facilitate the process of transformation; they are more detective than dictator. They question, gather information, observe their clients' reactions, analyze the data for patterns and clues, and draw conclusions based on what they observe and are told. While their ultimate goal is similar (presumably not assigning guilt), their methodology is different—though, hopefully, respectful and kind.

Clients provide the information and deserve to collaborate in the healing process. In fact, doing so empowers and encourages them. Whether we are patients, clients, or children in a family system, we all want to feel appreciated and that our contributions are valued. People tend to support what they help create. When families use unilateral hierarchies to make and enforce rules, the result is generally either resistance (resentment or revolution), or demoralization (despair or self-destructive habits). Neither approach teaches children life skills nor does it foster love and connection. Only mutually respectful resolution of difference and appreciation of intention can do that. The goal of Satir work is to help clients learn what they need to know to achieve their goals while creating loving and mutually satisfying relationships. That takes respectful facilitation and modeling of congruent behavior.

Therapist as Mentor, Model, Guide, Resource, and Detective

Satir believed that organic systems were healthier than hierarchical ones. She saw the therapist as a guide in a co-creation process. She empowered people to find and trust their own wisdom. In the following pages, I will describe a Satir-based model of therapy.

The Role of the Therapist

- Make contact
- See, hear and accept people
- Allow people to experience authentic concern and empathy
- Normalize their experience
- Invite them to share what they already know or have tried
- Model ways of uncovering authentic needs and wants
- Identify obstacles for getting needs met
- Evaluate coping skills
- Teach, model and apply new coping skills
- Support clients through the learning curve
- Coach clients how to understand and address outside resistance
- Reinforce practice and successes
- Define new possibilities.

The most effective therapists maintain an authentic and congruent presence so that clients will feel safe enough to disclose feelings, experiences and ideas that might be embarrassing or shame-filled. Progress in therapy correlates with the level of trust and connection the client forms with the therapist.

The Need for Mentors and Models

Our primary triad, Ma, Pa, Kid, as Satir called it, is our first mentorship. Sometimes older siblings, relatives, nannies, family friends or foster caregivers serve this purpose, too. Our first years of life are devoted to learning all we can from these people. Because learning begins well before we have language, we tend to learn more from what people do than what they tell us should be done.

In fact, modeling the behavior we want to see in our children is our most efficient way of teaching values and behaviors. An exception to this might be a blind child, or one with a developmental challenge who needs explicit teaching of skills as well as modeling, but in general, the best way to prove we value something is to match our words with our behaviors.

This Brothers Grimm story occurs in several forms in different cultures and illustrates the power of modeling:

The Old Man and his Grandson

There was once a very old man, whose eyes had become dim, his ears dull of hearing, and his knees trembled. When he sat at table he could hardly hold the spoon and spilt the broth upon the table-cloth or let it run out of his mouth. His son and his son's wife were disgusted at this, so the old grandfather at last had to sit in the corner behind the stove, and they gave him his food in an earthenware bowl, and not even enough of it. And he used to look towards the table with his eyes full of tears. Once, too, his trembling hands could not hold the bowl, and it fell to the ground and broke. The young wife scolded him, but he said nothing and only sighed. Then they bought him a wooden bowl for a few half-pence, out of which he had to eat.

They were once sitting thus when the little grandson of four years old began to gather together some bits of wood upon the ground. "What are you doing there?" asked the father. "I am making a little trough," answered the child, "for father and mother to eat out of when I am big."

The man and his wife looked at each other for a while, and presently began to cry. Then they took the old grandfather to the table, and henceforth always let him eat with them, and likewise said nothing if he did spill a little of anything.

Children best absorb the lessons they are shown. Telling children not to steal isn't nearly as effective as having them see us go out of our way to return extra change from the store.

Saying one thing and then doing another is the best way to teach children the opposite of what we intend.

> *One parent-educator demonstrates how much actions speak louder than words by telling her audience: "Put your finger on your nose." As she says it, however, she puts her own finger on her chin; almost universally audience participants put their finger on their chin.*

Therapists teach by modeling as well. It is one reason that Satir created her Satir Family Camp, which still exists after 35 years. She felt that therapists must work out their own problems so that they won't model poor behavior for their clients and families. Satir Family Camp is a week-long intentional community where families observe and practice positive life and parenting skills. The young adults who grew up attending the camp tend to be more friendly, well-balanced, ethical, socially conscious, respectful, trusting and mentally healthy human beings—maintaining healthy relationships and families. So far, Satir's vision was an astounding success.

Sometimes a parent models how not to be:

> *A young mother named Melinda describes how she learned to be truthful when she was five years old: Melinda's mother, Ruth, did not want her own mother, Grandma Rose, to come to Melinda's fifth birthday party. Ruth told Grandma Rose that no event was planned—a lie to avoid inviting her. Weeks later, Grandma Rose asked Melinda what she had done for her fifth birthday. Forgetting the lie, she described the party; Melinda was then punished by both Grandma Rose (for excluding her) and Ruth (for getting her in trouble by **telling the truth!**) Fortunately, Melinda took away the meaning that lying was terrible and would ultimately result in misery and injustice.*

We can also consciously sculpt the behaviors we want to see in our children.

> *Truthfulness and honesty were always very important to me. While I am very diplomatic, I answer even difficult questions accurately, and take responsibility for my mistakes. I consciously reinforced honesty in my children by giving them a reduced punishment for admitting a crime, and letting them keep a second allowance if they pointed out when I'd accidentally paid them twice in the same week. When there is little or no advantage to bad behavior, children generally avoid it.*

The therapist similarly should model and reinforce effective, desirable behaviors. Satir consistently modeled the behaviors she was trying to teach; she practiced excellent communication skills, behaved congruently with her clients, and demonstrated positive appreciation, authentic empathy and real concern. Whatever the therapeutic issue, we cannot heal or learn how behaving differently feels, unless the therapist provides the example in a safe environment.

> *JJ had trouble trusting people because as a child his parents would get drunk and hurt him. He would stay away from people for fear of being hurt. It took years of kind treatment by his therapist to overcome his fear that people would hurt him if they could.*

While therapy has become more accepted in the last decade, there are still many who feel that we should be able to solve our own problems. Some communities provide wonderful support systems through religious institutions, schools, or extended family. But most of us depend upon mentors and role models to learn how best to navigate life. When asked if we remember our favorite teachers, we easily describe the people who most inspired, understood and encouraged us. We also remember our worst teachers, those who made life miserable for us day after day. We all need positive models to see and guide us.

> *My most important mentor is Dr. Linda Silverman, now an international expert on gifted children and adults. She was a 6th grade school teacher when I met her; I was twelve years old. Her acceptance and appreciation of my gifts continue to allow me to take risks and work towards achieving my own highest and best purpose. Her modeling of a deep commitment to helping the gifted and improving the world has been a lifelong inspiration. I was the first member of my family to attend college, let alone graduate school, but I always knew these efforts were part of reaching my goals. Linda Silverman's mentorship made that seem possible.*

If we have done a good job of modeling and building a strong foundation of esteem and judgment, our children will make good decisions, even about the mentors they choose to emulate. While there are no guarantees, if we populate our lives with people we admire and trust, who also model what we value, our children have a better chance of creating a productive and happy life for themselves.

There is no formula for finding mentors, good people are everywhere. When we open our hearts to finding someone, we often do. One of my clients found his first mentor when he was arrested and had to serve several months in a juvenile detention facility; one guard encouraged him to make a better life, and now he is a successful entrepreneur with a happy family. Others credit their AA sponsors for having saved and inspired them. Many describe influential relatives, such as a grandfather or uncle who encouraged and supported them in a meaningful way. A mentor is someone willing to "pay forward" the kindness, guidance, and support they received at critical times in their own lives.

One obstacle to finding trustworthy resources is that we're not trained to look for them in the right places. In the United States, self-sufficiency is rewarded, dependence shunned. Other cultures honor the wisdom of the aged, even when they become dependent. Instead of teaching our children the real values they might want in a role model, we elevate high income (sports or entertainment icons) or powerful people (politicians or CEOs) into heroes. They may or may not hold any of our core values, and often turn out to have "feet of clay" when their private indiscretions become public.

The best mentors share more than values with us; they see our potential and believe in our ability to fulfill it. Many of my clients are highly gifted; for them, it is important to have a mentor or therapist who understands what is typical of a person with a high IQ, and who has a tolerance for the existential conflicts they experience. If we tend to be sensitive and emotional, we need someone who is empathic and has learned how to maximize their sensitivities and feelings to successfully navigate the world. Most problems are only difficult in a particular context. Our optimal mentor is someone who can help us achieve success in challenging environments, while guiding us toward finding rewarding ones that are a better fit.

Some Possible Sources of Good Mentors

Families	**Friends**
Teachers	**Community leaders**
Clubs	**Publications**
Spiritual centers	**Schools**
Extended family	**Referrals from others**
Jobs	**Internet**

The Therapist as Detective

The therapist is always gathering information in order to better understand the client. She uses that information to help the client understand patterns, identify challenges, set goals etc. When she does this, she is also modeling ways of getting to know others in meaningful and deep ways. Without this information about the client, she cannot fully understand what her clients need and how to help them.

> **Some Questions the Therapist/Detective Needs to Ask:**
> - Why has this individual sought therapy?
> - What is his or her personal story?
> - What events have brought her to this point?
> - What are the obstacles to doing what she wants to do?
> - What has she tried in the past and how effective has that strategy been?
> - Where did his or her belief system originate?
> - What is the perspective of other family members?
> - Are there learning style differences in the family?
> - Are there personality style differences?
> - Does the individual have a hidden disability?
> - Is there unrecognized giftedness?
> - What are the person's strengths?
> - What resources and support systems exist?
> - What might happen if the individual/couple/family tried this new idea?
> - What does she think might make a difference?

Therapists, Techniques and Interventions

Most therapists use a variety of tools and techniques to best understand their clients. Therapists may gain the information about us by using quantitative tools, such as IQ tests and inventories, or qualitative means, such as conversation and observation. Regardless of the toolkit, real progress comes from the relationship that grows while therapists apply the information they have gleaned.

Under optimal conditions, the therapeutic process is a testing ground for new practices and ways of our being in the world. Ideally, it is the place where old wounds are healed so we can move ahead without old burdens weighing us down. The therapist (a) helps us to understand

and release old habits, (b) models potential new behaviors, and (c) allows us to practice the new behaviors in safety. Eventually, the more effective behavior becomes the norm.

Studies of therapeutic outcomes indicate that methodology is less important than relationship between therapists and clients. If the therapeutic relationship is one of trust, good boundaries, and appropriate attachment, therapy is more likely to help. The therapist must have the necessary training and skill to select the appropriate treatment, but personality and chemistry also make a big difference. And it is up to the therapist to establish good boundaries.

Therapeutic Tools and Techniques

I use a variety of techniques depending upon the individual's, couple's, or family's needs. Qualitative approaches are especially useful, particularly in the beginning, to help clients focus their thoughts and provide a benchmark for assessing progress. I use diagnostic tools, like the *Myers-Briggs Personality Type Inventory*, with couples and families; some of the personality differences it identifies help me to understand people and quickly identify the source of their conflicts. Inevitably, as I give the family their results, the response is "that explains a LOT!" Consciousness usually precedes behavior change, and it certainly helps change attitude.

Qualitative discussions and observations both with the family, and individually with each member, help me understand the dynamics of the family system. This inventory and its implications will be discussed in detail in later chapters.

I apply Virginia Satir's models and techniques with people of all ages. Chronological age can be misleading since people function at different maturity levels under different circumstances. Additionally, the gifted demonstrate significant asynchronous development (sometimes emotionally younger than their years would predict, but intellectually much older). Satir's model often provides both diagnostic information and material for insight and change.

A Genogram illustrates the genealogy of the family depicting relationships of family members such as marriages, divorces, deaths, births, and ages. A Family Map is a type of Genogram that includes other information about the history or experience of the family. It may include a life chronology that describes significant events, notes about the nature of a relationship (such as ones that are emotionally or physically too close, cut-off, supportive, or critical). It can include statements, descriptions, facts, opinions, or feelings about family members, as well as messages or gifts that person provided. Both types of illustrations are useful when trying to understand and reveal underpinnings of current family dynamics and patterns.

Example Family Map (Genogram) Illustrating Emotional Cut-Off
(Arrows indicate those family members who don't speak to each other)

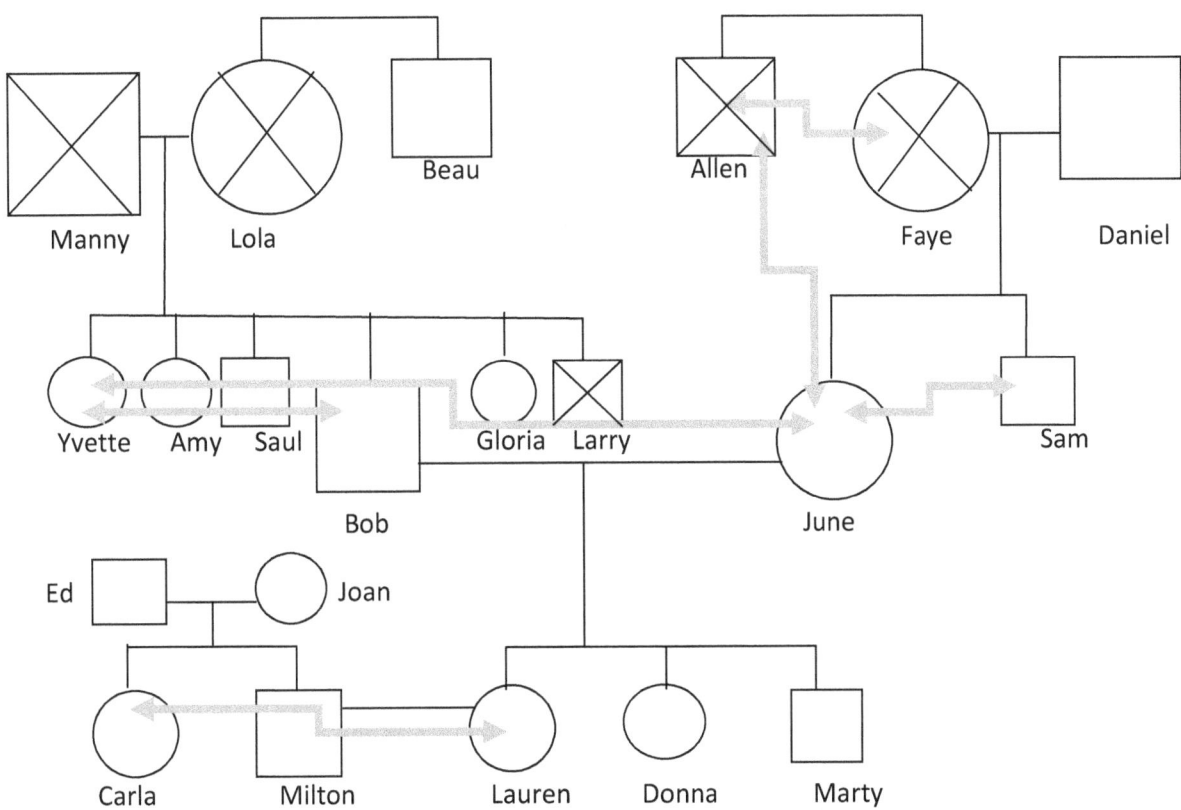

Family Sculpture, another tool, visually illustrates relationships by posing family members interacting. This process can quickly accomplish more insight than many sessions of traditional therapy. However, no amount of diagnostics will take the place of the therapist personally experiencing the client directly revealing who she is and what is important to her.

Example of a Family Sculpture

Family Sculpture by college age daughter showing how she feels far away and how she sees her parents as absorbed with each other, with the father in a dominant role.

The Therapist's Use of Self in Therapy

While some therapeutic schools admonish therapists not to reveal anything about themselves or their experiences and feelings to their clients, Satir shared her own life challenges as part of the therapeutic process. A graduate degree and license to practice proves professional training, but life experience can provide invaluable life lessons. Nothing can guarantee wisdom, or even skill, but knowing a helping professional has surmounted similar challenges can provide hope in darkness. Often disclosures also increase connection and serve to reduce the shame that keeps the client from being candid and living life joyfully. The barometer of disclosure is whether the information is relevant and useful. If a therapist chooses to disclose information about her personal experience, stories should be brief and contain a relevant point or concept.

While I use examples of things I've learned from my own life, particularly in raising my three children, metaphors, jokes or anecdotes about the subjects we address are also effective. When parents ask my qualifications, I sometimes respond that the most important one is raising three children who all turned out to be wonderful human beings. I believe a big reason twelve-step programs work is that sponsors are real people who have struggled and overcome similar problems. They share their mutual challenge and experience, as well as the solutions that worked for them. This inspires hope in the listener.

My most valuable lessons come from life experience, both my own, and those of my clients. Satir often discussed her own life and how she learned what she knew. She maintained that we connect through our similarities and grow though our differences. How can one do either if the therapist is a blank slate?

If the client asks a direct question about something, I evaluate my potential response by considering a number of therapeutic concerns, such as "What does the client need to learn?" "Will the disclosure promote deeper trust?" "Could it hurt the therapeutic alliance?" "How will he or she use the answer?" "Will knowing this information further the therapeutic process?" Ultimately, my response depends on what the client needs in that moment and for the future.

Illustrating a concept remains one of the best ways of introducing a new possibility. In describing various ways I and others have resolved a problem, the client receives several new possible ways to handle a challenge. When it comes to parenting ideas, I may start with the relevant research. But, I find that sharing a particular strategy drawn from concrete experience is more convincing and relevant than data and theory. What is most important is to understand that there are all kinds of therapists, and clients, as consumers, have a right to select one whose experience, personality and theoretical orientation match their needs.

Chapter Two: Helpers 29

Worksheet for Chapter 2: Resources

Question: *Who are your resources?*

Activity: *Make a sun with you at the center, and rays of sunshine showing who your mentors, models, and guides have been, and what you have learned from each of them.*

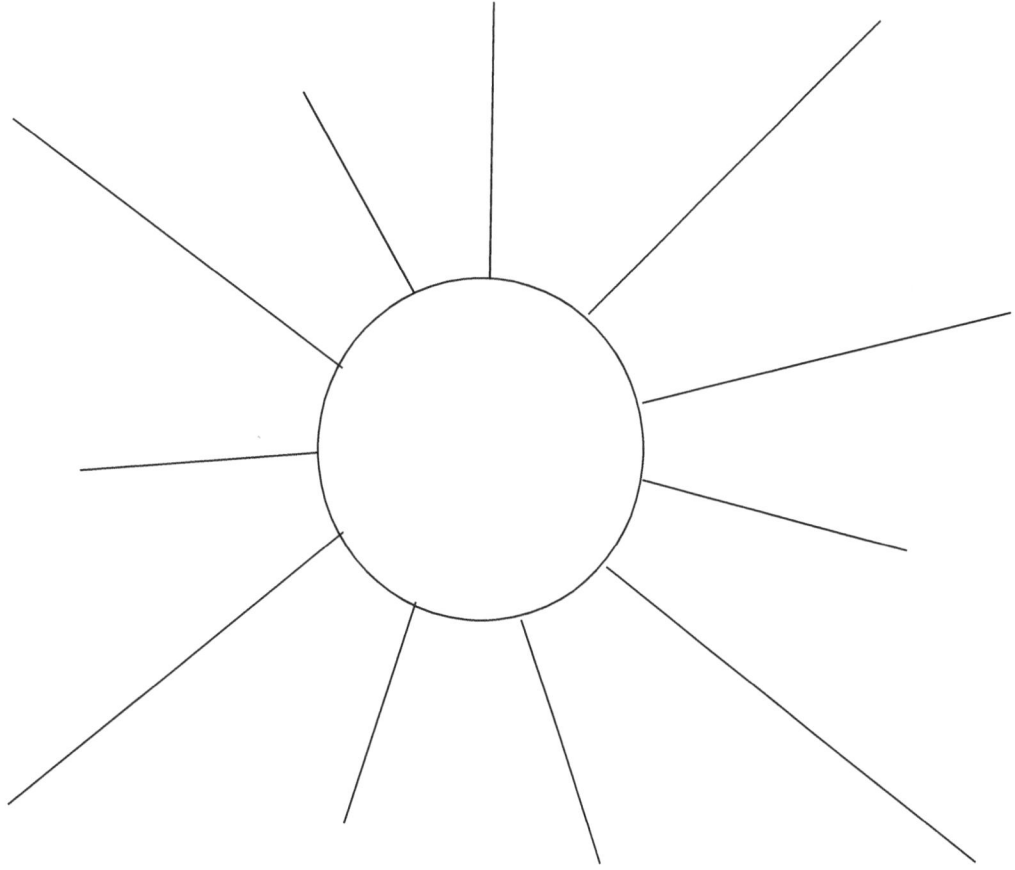

Challenge: *Call one of them this week and reconnect. Tell them what they have meant to you and that you appreciate their support.*

Part Two: New Information

"There are four areas of problems in families: self-worth, communication, rules, and link to society (how people relate to others outside the family)"   –Virginia Satir

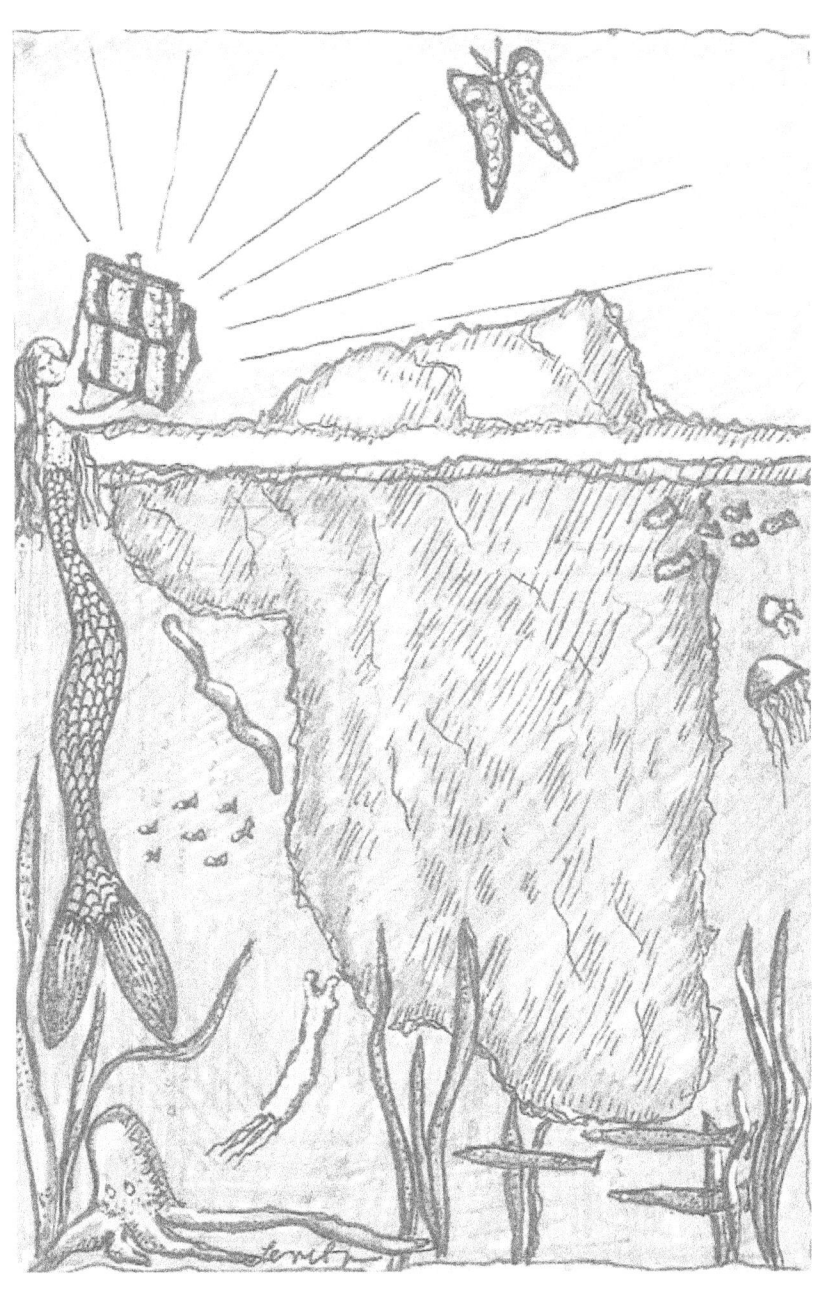

Chapter Three: Connection

"Allow yourself to become intimately connected with all your parts: so free, to have options and to use those options freely and creatively; to know that whatever was in the past was the best that we could do, because it represented the best we knew at the time; it represented the best in our consciousness.

As we move toward knowing more, being more conscious, we also then become more connected with ourselves. And in connecting with ourselves, we can form connections with others."
— *Virginia Satir*

Improving awareness and appreciation of the Self is an early goal for most therapeutic work. If we are not accepting of *who* we are, it is very difficult to keep our hearts open to hearing anything new. We may look to others to define us as okay. Or we might only feel valuable if we are accomplishing something. Many gifted and talented individuals receive high praise for what they *do*; they forget that what they *are* is really what allows them to do anything. Some of us learn that what we think about ourselves isn't as important as what others think; some learn the opposite and only trust their own opinion of themselves. Obviously, this topic is important when the goals are healing old wounds and building fulfilling relationships. How can we have a healthy relationship with someone else, if our relationship to our Self is critical, punitive, perfectionistic and rejecting?

> *Amy's father was critical and judgmental. He found something wrong with everything she did. In contrast, her mother praised everything she did without exception. From this contrast, Amy learned only to trust her own perception and valuation of her work. While useful in some ways, it hobbled her ability to take guidance or feedback seriously and ultimately hurt her career and relationships.*

As Satir maintained, parents do the best job they can, given their own experiences and limitations. Still, even if we had the greatest parents in the world, life experience can batter our self-esteem enough to undo even the most supportive and nurturing early experiences. Fortunately, positive early support helps most of us to be at least somewhat resilient when we face the "slings and arrows of outrageous fortune" or just mean people.

Most people, however, have wounds from their family of origin that affect their functioning in every other part of their lives. Some are wounds that came from childish meanings (for example, a parent is depressed, the child may magically believe he or she has caused it or is deficient for not being able to "fix" it). Some come from direct messages when overwhelmed or ignorant parents are hypercritical or abusive.

Children make meanings and draw conclusions based on immature understanding and judgment. Their parents might not understand their needs, or they might be self-absorbed and incapable of fulfilling the child's needs. Often the initial focus of therapy revolves around healing wounds that insecure or dysfunctional attachments created. The quality of the relationship with the therapist is part of that healing process because the therapist is modeling authentic and empathetic responses, and re-parenting the client so that she can move on through the phases of emotional development.

The concept of "New Information" addresses how the therapeutic connection is built and how it is essential to achieve growth and practice the skills necessary to achieve goals. The therapeutic relationship is both a place to relearn and correct unhelpful bad habits, and a place to practice new, healthier ones. It should be a safe environment, where we feel that our best interest is always being considered and we are being empowered through education and encouragement.

When we speak of connection, we tend to think about connections with others. That is a focus of later chapters, since making contact and achieving intimacy are usually important life goals. Before we can connect with others, we must be able to look inside and meet the needs of our own internal emotional system—yearnings, feelings, motivations, confidence. Until we gain enough insight to appreciate the unique gifts we have to offer others, it is difficult to have the courage to reach out to others.

Connecting to Self

When I talk about successfully connecting to the Self, I am talking about a two-part process. Knowing your Self, the first part, requires awareness and consciousness; insight is also useful. This is where a therapist can help. The therapist should be able to give feedback, guide our inner search, and give us tools to help us stay present and be mindful of inner experiences. The second is accepting and loving *who* you are. These are the feelings about the person you discovered in the first part. Knowing your Self is important, accepting and cherishing that person is even more so. Often this means relating to our Self-criticism in a more healthy way.

Connecting to Your Self

Step One: Know thyself
- Who are you?
- What is great about you?
- What is unique about you?
- What do you like?
- What do you want to change?

Step Two: Accept and love who you are
- How do you feel about your Self?
- How do you treat your Self?
- If you could see yourself as others do, what would you think?
- What messages do you (or others) give you about you?
- What do you say to your Self? Are you kind?
- When (if ever) have you really loved yourself?

The next few chapters will provide specific guidelines for helping us appreciate our Selves more fully. Accepting and loving what we see is a process that requires challenging the blame, shame and judgment that prevents self-acceptance and self-love.

Achieving Consciousness
- Analyze like a detective in a "who dunnit..."
- Observe and evaluate like an anthropologist studying a culture.
- Solicit opinions and feedback from family and friends.
- Join a group and solicit observations from strangers.
- Meditate on what you need to know to understand yourself.
- Journal using your non-dominant hand to access unconscious thoughts.
- Ask your parents and siblings for memories to deconstruct for clues.

We may have difficulty knowing what is real about our Selves. We may believe certain things, while our behaviors reveal something different from our beliefs. If we have problems connecting and maintaining long-term relationships, this may be a direct result of presenting an inauthentic Self to the world. If we do this too long or too often, we actually forget what is beneath the façade the world sees. Or, if we developed this persona at a very young age, we might not even know what is real and what is a survival mechanism, potentially outdated and unnecessary.

We all develop a public self that we project to the world. It protects our vulnerabilities and projects what, up to that time, we found was a winning strategy. But is it still? Often an old strategy that worked in a family of origin stops working, or never worked outside of the family. Evaluation is both useful and necessary.

> *The comedian, Brian Regan, jokes about growing up in a large family where it was necessary to "call" objects in order to claim them as his own. This strategy did not work when he began school. "I call that chair!" His teacher responded, "Brian, everyone calls that 'chair.'"*

Obstructions to a Healthy Relationship with Self and Others

- 'It's not my fault….."
- "Everything bad happens to me…"
- "I'll never let them see me."
- "I'll be what they want me to be."
- "How dare they….?"
- "Who cares?"
- "No one would like me anyway."
- "I can manipulate them and get anything I want."
- "I deserve…." or "I don't deserve…"
- "No one would ever want to be with me."
- "If I just…., maybe they will like me."

Sometimes relationships are doomed by expectations; or we accept a negative image or role: "The Difficult One" of the family, "The Easy-Going One," "The Peacemaker," "The Achiever." Each of these defines us (whether positively or negatively) and allows others to limit our sense of Self. Breaking out of the role we've been assigned is not always easy, especially if it has become a part of our identity (even though it may never have fit). That's why it is so important to know, connect and accept our Selves *before* we try to connect with others. People with a history of unstable and unfulfilling relationships are often the most blind to their role in creating them.

In later chapters, I will discuss tools for understanding and correcting unhelpful expectations. For now, know that looking inward and making sense of what we see are necessary to create positive relationships with others, as well as achieve inner peace.

Most of us need help gaining insight because we all have inevitable blind spots. This is where a good therapist is essential.

> *Janet was "The Pretty One" in the family. Her sister Joan was "The Smart One." When Janet turned 30, she became very depressed because she noticed a wrinkle. In therapy she began to detach her sense of worth from the role she'd accepted in childhood. Up to that point her life decisions had conformed to the role her family assigned her. She had dropped out of high school to become a model, married young, divorced and obtained a job as an administrative assistant.*
>
> *After exploring her interests and achievements, she began to see that she had excellent business instincts. Eventually she asked her boss to pay for her to go back to complete her degree. To her surprise, she turned out to be an exceptional student. She went on to complete her MBA and take an executive position with the company that had supported her through school. With her confidence restored, she found a partner who appreciated who she was as a whole...wrinkles and all.*

How to Transform Blind Spots into Insights

Most people learn something about who they are at an early age, from family and peers. Regardless of how accurate the labels may be at a given time, they rarely define a whole person and our real experiences. Additionally, the person projecting the attributes might have an ulterior motive, such as competitiveness, control, manipulation (to get the person to do more of something or less of it), etc.

However, we earn these labels from people who may or may not be reliable or competent to judge us. Depending upon their own expectations and prejudices, they may project their feelings onto their children (or other people's children). We, however, as children listening to the adults we presumed love us, believe them at some deep level. These labels can influence us throughout life.

Additionally, people know their own intentions and purpose, but they cannot always see their behaviors through the eyes of others. Some of us have no better understanding of our own choices and reactions than we do of others'. This is one reason that therapists are sometimes at a disadvantage. They are dependent upon reports from people who may have limited awareness of themselves, and must draw conclusions based on one side of a distorted story. That is why we start with understanding our Self and then move on to how those insights might impact our relationships.

Labels That Can Limit Identity

Smart/ Dumb	**Responsible/Irresponsible**	**Out-going/Shy**
Moody/ Stable	**Friendly/Antisocial**	**Interesting/Boring**
Athletic/Clumsy	**Hard Working/Lazy**	**Pretty/Plain**
Strong/Weak	**Capable/Incompetent**	**Healthy/ Sickly**
Noisy/Quiet	**Musical/Tone-deaf**	**Organized/Messy**
Wise/Stupid	**Creative/Unimaginative**	

Tony came to therapy complaining that his horrible wife left him and took his children to her parents' home to live. He complained he can't understand why she would be doing this. He described his close-knit family, his friends, his successful business, and how his wife had turned his children against him. At the second session he described being arrested because his wife had seduced him, and then had him arrested for rape. His list of complaints spanned years, yet he wanted her back.

Upon further investigation, Tony described how his family considered him blessed—that he could do no wrong in their eyes. He complained that he had bad luck and that people had been "out to get him" his whole life. He also admitted that he had a "little temper," but only when driven to the limit by injustices perpetrated against him.

Eventually, Tony was jailed for the rape, and lost custody of his children. His grown sons testified against him, saying they had witnessed him physically abusing their mother.

Tony believed much of what he said. His early learning that he "could do no wrong" and that he was a victim, led him to justify doing whatever he wanted. His lack of insight made it impossible to avoid the negative consequences he eventually had to endure.

It can be challenging to accept the possibility that our experiences do not represent the whole picture. For many, the therapy office is the only place to check out the accuracy of a perception. First, there must be trust so that we don't discount the therapist's range of possible interpretations.

Positive Connection with a Therapist

Positive connection in therapy occurs when the therapist has created an empathic and accepting environment. Sometimes a therapist's acceptance of us (warts and all) will be enough to allow us to connect with deep trust, and even overcome our old feelings of guilt and shame. Sometimes we approach a therapist with an intuitive understanding that we can trust them.

> **Conditions for Client Trust**
>
> 1) **Belief in the good intentions of the therapist; that she or he**
>   - is a caring, well intentioned person
>   - is truthful
>   - speaks in the best interest of the client
>   - cares about the client
>
> 2) **Confidence that the therapist's motivations are appropriate; that she or he**
>   - isn't trying to prolong the therapy to make more money
>   - isn't saying what the client wants to hear because she or he is being paid
>   - provides information that is useful to the client
>
> 3) **Satisfaction with the therapist's wisdom and training; that she or he**
>   - has the appropriate training
>   - is skilled at applying what she has learned
>   - is insightful enough to give credible possible outcomes
>   - understands her clients and their needs accurately
>   - can follow the clients' thought processes
>   - has suggestions that are useful, relevant and easy to apply.

When there is good connection with the therapist, there is a positive feeling about the therapeutic interaction, even if it involves painful work. This is because we no longer feel alone.

Positive Connections in the World

A positive connection to the world is the extension of feelings of connection developed in the therapeutic environment to the outside world. Two or more people feel trust, empathy, and caring about each other. They feel mutually understood and comfortable about sharing thoughts or feelings. When this meeting of minds or spirit occurs (not just with a romantic interest, but with anyone—friends, family, co-workers) there is a sense of hope and confidence.

We each have our own strategies for achieving connection and our own set of reasons that might allow us to feel connected to one person and distanced from another. Usually good communication is the best way to begin and maintain connection; being connected to your Self is the best way to start that process.

First Step to Connecting with the Self

Start with the exercise at the end of this chapter. It provides a set of parts that can be verified with family, friends, or your therapist. Once we have a picture of *who* we are—which of our traits or skills serve us best, which ones block us—we can begin to form a picture of what assets we bring to a relationship. Next comes an evaluation—are these traits representative of who we really are or of who we really want to be. We may decide that some things on that list are not true, or not representative, or not in our best interest going forward. That is the start of a personal journey, and an individual treasure map for growth, success, and happiness.

Feelings of Connection

Trust	Confidence
Reliability	Understanding
Comfort	Caring
Calm	Dependability
Acceptance	Inner Peace

Connectedness with Self and Others

by Virginia Satir

Allow yourself to become

Intimately connected

With all your parts.

So free, to have options

And to use those options

Freely and creatively.

To know that whatever

Was in the past

Was the best that we could do,

Because it represented the best we knew.

It represented the best in our consciousness.

As we move toward knowing more,

Being more conscious,

We also then become

More connected with ourselves.

And in connecting with ourselves,

We can form connections with others.

Worksheet for Chapter 3: Connection

Question: *What do you know about your Self?*

Activity: *Create a parts party for your personality parts—either draw the parts and name them (i.e., give them lines to say) or just draw labels and name the parts. When you are done, go back and rate them for percentage helpful vs. percentage gets-in-the-way-of-growth.*

E.g., Curiosity - 60% helpful, 40% annoying

"It is helpful when I have clarified a situation, but annoying if I ask questions at inappropriate times; in the future I could be less annoying if I become more conscious of timing when asking a question."

Challenge: *Think of ways to appreciate and use the positive aspects of this part and to change or tone down the negative ones.*

Chapter Four: Contact

"When I can see, hear, understand, and touch another person, I feel contact has been made."
— Virginia Satir

We all have aspects ("parts") of ourselves that combine to make up who we are. Once we have connected with all the parts of our Self, we are ready to make contact with others. One of the reasons for connecting with all of our parts is that we know what we bring to the table when making contact with the outside world. It's like a store doing an inventory: if the store doesn't know what it has in stock, it can't accurately advertise or find what customers want. Not knowing what you have to offer or how to find it is a good way to lose business and opportunities. In relationships, it means you cannot fully connect.

We all have more and less socially adept parts. If the less helpful parts get in the way of making contact, it is up to us to find ways to transform them into useful resources. *Better listening skills can turn an unhelpful trait into one that contributes.*

Satir felt that it made more sense to *add parts* than to subtract them. For one thing, in the past it was probably useful for that part to do its job. For another, it is still a part of you—demonizing any part causes the old problem of guilt and shame, which makes it difficult to accept and love your Self. And it is much more difficult to *stop* doing something than to substitute a more positive behavior for an ineffective one. Just try to stop thinking of an Elephant.

The trick is to take traits that are no longer useful and either give them a new function, or retire them knowing they would be available if you ever needed them again.

> *Jo Ann smoked cigarettes most of her adult life. By the time her mother unexpectedly died, she hadn't touched a cigarette in years. Yet, as soon as her difficult sisters came to town for the funeral, she recognized the familiar craving. Instead of shaming herself for "backsliding," she identified a resentment/guilt cycle that upset her deeply whenever she was around them; she also noticed that smoking relieved those uncomfortable feelings. Once she understood that her smoking served a reasonable purpose, she could focus on improving her relationships with different coping strategies (instead of sending up smoke signals). Her cravings disappeared quickly.*

The Detective Strategy
Questions for Transforming an Obsolete Part

Example: a "Curious Part" is annoying 40% of the time

1) **What is it about this part that gets annoying?**
   - Do we ask too many questions too soon?
   - Do we ask inappropriate questions?
   - Do we forget to stop and listen to the answers?
   - Do we use the answers to say off-putting things?

2) **What could this part do differently?**
   - Should we plan questions before asking?
   - What listening skills could make it unnecessary to ask as many questions?
   - Do we need to know all the answers right now?
   - Do we need more patience so that the answers might come on their own?

3) **What contributions does this part make to a conversation?**
   - Can this skill be improved?
   - Is there another part that could be added to help this one be less annoying?

Your Relationship to Self and Contact with Others

When we don't appreciate who we are, we tend to hold back or wear a mask in the world. This is a reasonable response; it is difficult to trust others if we cannot trust ourselves. The mask acts as protection against being hurt. But it also acts as a wall when trying to make positive contact. This is why accepting and appreciating your Self is a critical step to becoming authentic in the world.

Sometimes we learn to wear a mask from our family of origin. Families with a lot of secrets and shame tend to discourage openness. "We don't air our dirty linens in public" is often the family rule, especially in families with substance or physical abuse. Even if we are free to be authentic within the family system, having to pretend normalcy in the outside world becomes more and more difficult as we expand our range of contact.

When we go out into the world and see that other people and families are different from ours, we begin the process of differentiation. Differentiation allows us to decide how we want to be in the world, even if it is very different from the way we responded in childhood. Unfortunately, the more closed and secretive the family of origin, the less differentiation is fostered. The more dysfunctional the family of origin, the more likely it is to keep the child attached (enmeshed) as long as possible.

> *Andrea entered therapy guiltily. The reason she came was that she was failing her college math class. At 30, she hadn't dated in six years, lived with her parents, and suffered the aches and pains of a woman triple her age. Her mother was very narcissistic, and her father was so dependent that he would not do anything without his wife's permission. Everything in her family of origin seemed to be about her mother. Critical and punitive, mom would purposefully compare Andrea and her siblings unfavorably, forcing them to compete for her attention and approval. Andrea grew up feeling incompetent, not even smart enough to finish college. She had married out of high school, but her mother had not liked her husband, and within a year Andrea divorced and moved back home.*
>
> *In therapy, Andrea identified her gifts and practiced building connection with her therapist. She gained self-confidence and began to experience success by challenging her old beliefs about being inadequate. As she practiced being authentic in the world, she started dating and eventually moved into an apartment with the man she later married.*

Identifying Positive Contact

As in Satir's quote, being able to see, hear and understand another person goes a long way toward creating contact with others. There are concrete skills we can learn in order to become better at letting people know us. All the understanding in the world doesn't aid connection unless the person knows we are doing it.

> *Whenever Jim had a fight with his wife, the next day he would take her car to get washed. His wife spent the next day baking his favorite dinner. Unfortunately, they neglected to tell each other the thoughtful gestures were a peace offering meant to repair the damage done by the fight. It wasn't until their divorce, while they were berating each other for never making up after a fight, that they discovered the intentions behind the actions. Their lack of communication completely undermined their efforts to rebuild connection after it was broken.*

Using Conversation to Make Contact

One purpose of conversation is to make contact, so it is wise to select relevant, significant, and mutually interesting topics to discuss, especially in an initial meeting. The conversation skills described below may seem basic, but it is surprising how often people forget some part of the process: they ask a question, but don't listen to the answer. Or they listen to the answer, but forget to make sure they understood or clarified what was meant. Or instead of keeping a comment relevant to the other person's communication, they change the subject or rush into a disclosure of their own—as if they were just waiting for the chance to hijack the conversation and make it be about them. Another problem might be attentional: getting distracted, looking around the room instead of at the speaker. All of these reactions are an impediment to making contact. If we don't make contact, we can't expect to achieve a real connection with another person.

The number of people in the conversation will also dilute the ability to make contact, especially if one is more loquacious or extraverted. Sometimes people who tend to be more introverted will partner with someone who is more socially extraverted. While this provides some relief around making initial contact, and even in carrying the conversation, it actually impedes one's ability to connect. Everyone needs to connect with at least one other person, whether it is a family member, a life partner, a friend or a business relationship. Longevity may even be a function of social connection. Real friendship enriches both parties. Life without positive connection may not seem worthwhile.

Every type of communication is more effective if it is individualized and demonstrates knowledge of the other person. Occasionally I have had clients who have significant communication problems. The condition called Asperger Syndrome (AS) is an example of a genetic predisposition to miss information important for communication and connection. While the newest version of the *Diagnostic Statistical Manual of Mental Disorders* (DSM-V) is moving AS into the Autism Spectrum category, I have seen significant differences between AS and autism. Autistic individuals appear less in need of connection with others. My experience is that "Aspies" (an affectionate term many use to refer to themselves and others) really want to connect, but that they need detailed instructions on how to manage it effectively. Often they don't notice or know how to interpret nonverbal cues. As teens, they may not know how to judge when to stop teasing, or when a joke isn't funny, when they are being too disclosing, offensive or when to stop arguing; these deficits can get them into trouble in every part of their lives. Basic skill training may not make them experts at connecting, but it can help keep them out of trouble.

The following chart of conversation skills can serve as a guide for parents to teach the fine art of conversation to their children, for anyone entering the helping professions, for teen social skills groups, for individuals who struggle with social interaction, and for anyone who wants to fine tune communication skills or support a socially inept part of the Self when tuning into other people.

Even without Asperger Syndrome, people are often ineffective at navigating certain social situations. In later chapters I discuss the elements of communication that foster contact, such as considering the needs of the Self, the Other and the Context. All these are necessary to communicate effectively. In this Chapter, I discuss several elements of connection, of which communication is only one. As soon as we have contact with another person, we have begun to create an atmosphere that may or may not result in connection.

Some Conversation Skills

1) **Consciously consider nonverbal cues:**
   - Stand or sit a comfortable distance away (notice if other person moves away)
   - Make eye contact
   - Loosely mirror body position/stance
   - Make sure facial expression is congruent with topic of conversation

2) **Ask questions about the other person's thoughts and feelings on a topic:**
   - What do you think about…?
   - How do you feel about…?
   - What led you to conclude…?

3) **Respond to answers in ways that show you've been listening:**
   - When you said…, it helped me understand…
   - Let me make sure I understood that…
     What I heard you say was…
   - So, you think/feel/hope…

4) **Ask clarifying follow-up questions:**
   - Can you explain more about why…?
   - Would you be willing to tell me more about…?

> ### Conversation Skills (continued)
>
> 5) **Offer short connecting disclosures that relate to the current discussion:**
>   - I feel that way when……..
>   - I've often thought that, too….
>   - I've had that experience myself…
>
> Caveat: You must be genuinely interested to connect to other people.

Emotional Banking Account:
Our Personal and Interpersonal Banking System

Before any contact occurs, we all start with what I term *Emotional Bank Accounts - EBAs*. These accounts function like actual bank accounts with balances, credits and debits, based on how we feel about ourselves and others. Completely subjective, the balance in our EBAs fluctuates depending upon our feelings about Self and Other. The currency of an EBA might be called "Good Will Units." Good Will Units include all the factors that contribute to our physical, mental and emotional health. Of course, this varies depending upon the interaction, our own mood and our individual needs, both in general and in the moment.

Sample of Subjective Units of Good Will Scale										
-100	-80	-60	-40	-20	0	+20	+40	+60	+80	+100
Enraged	Depressed	Hurt	Anxious	Sad	Neutral	Relaxed	Satisfied	Happy	Proud	Ecstatic

I talk about two types of accounts: Personal, which represent everything that is going on inside of us, and Interpersonal, which reflects our feelings about others. Each of us carries a Personal bank account, and many Interpersonal ones; each person we know has his or her own Interpersonal account, and even some exist for strangers, or classes of people, like "other drivers on the road" or "salespeople." If we have feelings about someone or something, we carry an EBA on that person or thing.

Presumably the closer the person is related to us, the more transactions that occur in the person's Interpersonal account. But proximity of relationship doesn't necessarily have a strong impact on the balance of an EBA, since some people in our lives co-exist with us peaceably, while others create extremes of emotional response.

Values of deposits in our Interpersonal accounts also vary based on the current balance of our Personal bank account. When we are in a bad mood, tired or sick, our Personal account might be empty or have a negative balance. All this affects how we relate to Self and Other.

Each person has different conditions that earn or spend Good Will. While generally this whole process occurs unconsciously, I find that consciously quantifying the Good Will of an interaction between +100 (really satisfying and positive) and -100 (highly dissatisfying and negative) helps people understand and communicate to others how thoughts and behaviors cause changes in our EBA balances. Both our Personal EBA balance (which depends upon the condition of the Self) and our Interpersonal EBA balances are constantly fluctuating depending upon a range of factors that affects each person differently.

Factors that Influence Balances in our Emotional Bank Accounts

Deposits		Withdrawals	
Physical Health	Exercise	Sleeplessness	Exhaustion
Joyfulness	Success	Illness	Pain
Approval	Appreciation	Rudeness	Criticism
Gratitude	Patience	Impatience	Annoyance
Forgiveness	Support	Gruffness	Arrogance
Help	Empathy	Patronization	Bullying
Acknowledgment	Recognition	Stereotyping	Put-downs
Spirituality	Inner Peace	Dishonesty	Abuse
Beauty	Nature	Failure	Sadness
Gifts	Thoughtfulness	Guilt	Shame
Surprises	Accomplishments	Disappointment	Overwhelm
Consideration	Kindness	Lack of Consideration	Meanness
Pride	Humor	Perfectionism	Anxiety

In this situation Good Will is defined as the individual subjective value that people consciously or unconsciously assign to their feelings about themselves (affecting the balance in their Personal EBA) and another person (affecting the balance in their Interpersonal EBA). All scores are subjective and based on individual perception. **Not** noticing your personal and interpersonal balances and how they are fluctuating can be a huge impediment to both current and future communication and connection. When I work with families, I begin by creating an EBA continuum with them so that they understand what their individual Good Will scale represents to them.

Good Will values are based on the perceptions and meanings each person makes of what they experience. Perceptions are based on what we learned in our families. They are a combination of beliefs (which are taught), values (which are the "shoulds" we internalize), and images (what we observed in our past.) They can vary broadly from individual to individual. We make meanings of what we experience based on these perceptions. The same statement can elicit a range of emotions depending upon the past and current relationship between the speakers, the current mood of the individuals, and feelings about the topic being discussed. Here are two possible conversations addressing a son, Bill, who has forgotten to take out the trash. Each approach has a different effect upon balances in the Personal and Interpersonal bank accounts.

> ***Sample Blaming Conversation (Bold = spoken words;** Italics = thoughts)*
> Context: Mom has headache. Bill is tired from school and is playing video games.
>
> **Mom: "Bill, you forgot to take out the trash again."**
> *Both think: "Poor me, I don't deserve to be treated this way"*
> **Bill: "I'm too tired, I'll do it later."**
> *Mom thinks: "He's lazy! This is so unfair"*
> *Bill thinks: "She never gives me a break; at least I stuck up for myself."*
> **Mom: "You NEVER remember when you say that. DO IT RIGHT NOW! "**
> *Mom thinks: "Am I am bad mother, or is he a bad kid?"*
> **Bill: "Fine, but I hate you."**
> *Mom thinks: "I don't deserve that. I can't wait until he moves out"*
> *Bill thinks: "I can't wait until I can move out"*

Our emotional reactions to conflict are influenced by many factors; in this case past experience with doing the chores in a timely fashion, asking for or having needs met in the past, and the starting condition of each Emotional Bank Account all affect how much this interaction will undo past positive conversations or experience.

We all have a range of possible responses to people and situations; these are based on our values, our past experiences and the current state of our self-esteem. Using this example, some of us don't have any reaction to being reminded of something we forgot to do; some of us are self-critical under the same circumstances; some resent being reminded; others are happy to get a reminder when they forget something they meant to do. All responses reflect both external and internal factors. This also affects the impact an event has on an Emotional Bank Account.

Sample Congruent Conversation (Bold = spoken words; *Italics = thoughts)*
Context: Mom has headache. Bill is tired from school and is playing video games.

Mom: "Bill, could you please take out the trash?"
    Mom thinks: "Bill's been really busy lately."
Bill: "Man, I forgot again; I'm sorry. I'll do it now." (Takes out trash)
    Bill thinks: "I need to find a better way to remember this."
Mom: "Thanks Bill. I appreciate that."
    Mom thinks: "I'm glad he took responsibility for forgetting. He means well."
Bill: "I will try to remember next week. You don't look too good; are you okay, Mom?"
    Bill thinks: "I hope she isn't mad because I forgot again."
Mom: "Oh, I just have a headache; it's not because of this."
    Mom thinks: "Bill is so perceptive and caring. I'm a lucky mom."
    Bill thinks: "I'm glad I checked about that; I wouldn't want to give her a headache because I messed up."
Bill: "You should rest, then. I'll make dinner tonight."
    Mom thinks: Wow, I must be doing something right. I didn't even have to ask him to help me."
    Bill thinks: "It's nice to be able to help her out once in a while. She's always nice to me."
Mom: "I'd really appreciate that. How thoughtful of you to offer. I'm proud you're my son."
    Bill thinks: "Mom's so nice. I even like helping; it makes up a little for forgetting my chore."

When people relate to each other in a congruent, respectful way, they build credibility and add to both their Personal and Interpersonal Emotional Bank Accounts. They feel better about themselves and about each other.

Worksheet for Chapter 4: Contact

Our Emotional Bank Accounts

Question: *What "Good Will" values would you assign your various feelings?*

Activity: *Fill in your feelings on the charts below.*

Personal Subjective Units of Good Will Scale

Score   *Possible Situation*   *Associated Feeling*

+100 _____

+80 _____

+60 _____

+40 _____

+20 _____

0 _____

-20 _____

-40 _____

-60 _____

-80 _____

-100 _____

Chapter Five: Growth

"The Third Birth, through the family and beyond, means when you have lived through the phase of apprenticeship, of being a human being in your family (of origin) and are now taking care of yourself as an adult, in this world, with opportunities and responsibility for continuing to evolve yourself, to allow yourself to let go of what you learned that no longer fits and give yourself permission to acquire and invent that which you now need. That is quite possible unless we keep ourselves trapped in the prison of how we were, or how we are supposed to be and are not." – Virginia Satir (Journals, pg. 135)

Understanding Family Of Origin (FOO)

Most of us look at our Family of Origin (FOO) with a critical eye. We identify traits we don't like about ourselves and search for a parent to blame for our faults; we often carry bitterness about the things our parents taught or failed to teach us, did or did not do. The idea that problems in adulthood can be traced back to childhood experiences is true—at least in part. Parents may be responsible for most of our early experiences, but good parenting doesn't assure perfect children and poor parenting doesn't guarantee failures.

Parents make a range of choices in the twenty-odd years it takes to raise us: values, beliefs, habits, rituals, discipline, and rules may or may not fit our needs or personalities. Parents may use a "one-size-fits-all" approach to parenting when siblings have very different needs. Most parenting choices mirror what was observed in their own childhood. This is called the "multi-generational transmission process" where behaviors (functional or otherwise) pass from generation to generation, regardless of the fit or function—as this old story illustrates:

> *Lisa was about to cook her first brisket for her new husband. Her husband watched admiringly as she carefully prepared it exactly like her mother and grandmother prepared it. The last step before putting it into the pan was to cut off the ends. Curious, her husband asked her what cutting off the ends did to help the recipe. Lisa realized she didn't know and quickly called to ask her mother. Her mother admitted, she also didn't know why they included that step, and said she would call her mother and find out. Everyone had a good laugh when Grandma admitted that the reason SHE cut off the ends was that her baking pan was too small to fit a whole brisket.*

Satir had a very practical philosophy for working with Family of Origin. She agreed that most of our problems begin with our FOO. She also felt that multi-generational patterns of behavior often acted as catalysts for dysfunctional behaviors. But, she maintained that all parents were "the best parents they knew how to be." This was a pretty audacious supposition—often vociferously refuted by victims of abuse and neglect. However, getting lost in a blame/bitterness cycle does little to allow healing or the chance to move on.

> *Tommy experienced an interesting form of neglect. Both he and his mother suffered from severe scoliosis, curvature of the spine. As his mother had aged, she'd suffered terrible pain and disfigurement as a result of the condition. She and her husband had more than enough money to pay for the surgery during the critical years that could have corrected the condition in her son, but they did nothing. As my client grew into adulthood, he had to suffer the consequences of this neglect; he struggled to understand how his mother could consign him to a life of pain. The family story was that his mother felt she'd had to suffer with the pain, and so should he. This explanation fit with other narcissistic aspects of her personality.*

> *I suggested another possible interpretation and Tom was visibly relieved. What if the surgery was dangerous and experimental at that time and Tom's mother succumbed to her fears for his life, over concerns for the alternative? She was a Holocaust survivor; what if she'd learned that survival, no matter how painful, was preferential to death. What if her reasoning was that if she could endure the pain of the scoliosis (not to mention her years in a Nazi work camp), then it would be better to have that burden than to risk her only son's death or worse disability by having an experimental operation? Also, when interpreted through the context of family members having been killed by the Nazis, wouldn't it make sense that she would cling to her child, knowing his imperfection was tolerable (since she had the same one)?*

> *This new interpretation brought relief for several reasons: Tom needed to believe his mother loved him, he wanted to believe his mother was a decent person who wouldn't wish pain on her only son, and he yearned to be able to love her without resentment. None of these could happen as long as he carried the blaming belief. This reframed possibility made room for forgiveness and his own sense of peace about his mother.*

It is easier to forgive parents for their mistakes if we can remember they are human beings with commensurate weaknesses and faults. Their experiences influenced what they did. We can never completely understand the reasons for their choices, because it is not possible to step into another person's shoes. But we have much to gain if we can grow to understand that they did the best that they could, given what they knew and believed at that time. Our parents can teach us how we want to be and how we want to raise our children, or they can teach us the opposite—what we need to avoid doing. It is our prerogative to make different choices when we parent our own children.

In some ways, the fact that any family is able to get along better than a randomly selected group of people is something of a mystery and a tribute to our ability to adapt and compromise. Children do not come with an owner's manual. There is a range of available advice (most of it generic) that presents itself as pressure from relatives, friends and community. Add to all of this the fact that children are constantly changing and it is easy to understand the confusion and insecurity parents feel. Also, some challenges are inherited; physical, social, mood and learning challenges can be genetically inherited. Even personality and behavior can have an in-born component, additional challenges parents may face.

Family relationships are filled with needs, expectations, feelings, hopes, wishes, and personality differences, not to mention the occasional health or happiness emergencies that pop up. Parents are expected to synthesize a huge amount of information. Some manage this better than others. We are all human and fallible.

Growth and Positive Intention

Blame and resentment are a barrier to growth. They focus on the source of the problem as external and inevitable. This stance leaves us powerless to grow—we are trapped by the fences of blame and resentment we've erected around ourselves. The facts are at least partially true, but staying bound by the past keeps us from reshaping the future.

In order to grow past blame and resentment, it is necessary to accept that your parents were the best parents they knew how to be. It's possible to see one's parents as flawed and still empathize with their positive intention. In fact, it is wise to try to see all people in that light (unless there is evidence to the contrary).

The next sections discuss positive intention and how negative behavior can spring from past hurt or from behaviors learned from our culture and parents' FOO; yet intention can still be positive. We cannot forgive our parents and move on until we accept the fact that hurtful behavior can come out of a positive intention (or that the negative intentions were the best the parent could do given the circumstances and their inner demons.)

> *In a Satir Family Reconstruction, Alice sculpted her grandfather's early life. He had been rejected by his stepfather and apprenticed as a virtual slave to a bricklayer at the age of six. There he was beaten and raped by the oldest son until he ran away at age 14. Living on his own, he made his way to the United States, contracted a loveless arranged marriage and raised two children, working fourteen hours a day as a bricklayer. At the end of the sculpt, when the role players gave feedback on their experience in that role, the man who'd played her grandfather was on the verge of tears. He said he had never felt such humiliation and hopelessness. While this didn't remove Alice's pain from having been molested by*

this grandfather, it allowed her to forgive the human being who'd been irreparably damaged before she'd even been born.

Positive Intention

Positive intention is an important concept: it is behavior that is inspired in the spirit of good will, and carried out in a non-judgmental way; it is not motivated by self-interest (although mutual interest, like a win-win outcome, could be a motivation). To move past the negative experiences of the past, it is necessary to believe that it is at least possible that a hurtful behavior was motivated by a neutral or positive intention. Whether we are dealing with perceptions of our childhood, our relationships, or making choices about our own behavior, finding a positive (or at least neutral) intention can significantly affect our beliefs and responses, and potentially heal old wounds.

It has been said that carrying around resentment and hate is like taking poison and expecting another person to die from it. We are the ones who die a little each time we re-experience the negative belief or feeling; each time we recount the negative story, we take an extra dose of poison.

> ### In Search of Positive Intention
> - Why would this person want to hurt me?
> - Is there any other possible explanation for their words or behavior?
> - Is there a minefield I might have accidently stepped into?
> - Could their behavior have a different interpretation?
> - Could there be something I don't know or they don't know?
> - Is there something I am meant to learn from this experience?
> - How do I remember this is one person and one event?
> - If this reminds me of past events, how will I remember this as only similar?
> - What can I do to avoid this happening in the future?

Belief in positive intention is an important foundation for building constructive family relationships. I have found that if I could find positive intention in a person's behavior, and ac knowledge this intention, it was easier for us to have a productive discussion. Conversely, if I could only find self-interest or negative intention in a person's behavior, I had little patience and less good will towards him or her. These conversations rarely went well. My adult children have shared that they did what was asked of them when they were growing up because they always believed that my request came from a place of positive intention, rather than out of a need to control them or out of self-interest.

Obstacles to Acknowledging Positive Intention

As human beings we feel with our hearts, and make meanings with our heads. When we get hurt, it is difficult to see past the pain we are feeling. Depending upon our resources—physical, emotional and spiritual—our sensitivity and resilience can vary from one minute to the next.

> **Maintaining Positive Intention is a Challenge**
> - when we are hurt;
> - when we feel "less than;"
> - when we feel emotions like envy, jealously, and greed;
> - when we are triggered by something that reminds us of past hurts;
> - when we believe others have negative intention towards us;
> - when we hold resentments, grudges, and want revenge for them;
> - when our personal emotional bank account is overdrawn.
>
> *Note: Everyone feels some or all of these at one time or another.*

Misguided Attempts at Expressing Positive Intention

Sometimes people don't know how to express positive intention effectively. This would include people who lack social skills (like diplomacy), or who are oblivious to people's reactions. When parents behave this way, children can learn negative behaviors or miss some positive connecting ones.

> *In Ellen's family, people used sarcasm to express humor. They teased each other with expressions like "No, duh" to show that a statement was obvious. Ellen said she knew her family had positive intention when they were sarcastic. However, in the wider world, sarcasm is often used as a put down or to express hostility. Ellen*

soon learned that most of the world did not respond well to her sarcasm, despite her personal positive intention.

Negative Intention / Displaced Hurt

Most violence—physical or emotional—is the result of displaced hurt. In some ways, feelings are not just about what is happening in this moment, but about what happened in the past, like an old broken bone being re-injured. Physical wounds heal more fully than emotional ones. Old emotional wounds may never fully heal. They can open and bleed at the approximation of a similar injury; this is when people are "triggered" by a similar displaced hurt.

> *While Abram was growing up, his mother would regularly enter his room and throw away anything she considered "trash." When she tossed his paper clip collection that he was saving, he was deeply upset, particularly since she did not apologize. As an adult, he would become enraged every time someone "touched his things." This over reaction felt punitive and unfair to his wife and children. He was still reacting to the wound that never healed over his paper clip collection.*

When our reaction to an event is out of proportion to the current experience, usually we are being triggered by a past hurt. A new, similar slight will re-open the wound and elicit an emotion that really belongs to the past experience, even though it is being expressed in the present.

A trigger response is like having a bruise. Getting bumped in a crowd might be annoying, but it doesn't warrant much notice. However, if a bruise is touched, even minimally, we recoil, yell, cry out, and maybe even punch back in response to the shock and pain caused by the hypersensitive bruise.

The Unfairness Reflex

Probably the most common example of a trigger reaction is what I call the Unfairness Reflex. This is when we experience a disproportionately strong response (anger or hurt) to an event that feels unfair. This Unfairness Reflex is relatively universal because everyone experiences unfairness at one time or another. If a child is deeply hurt by unfair treatment, each time something unfair happens in the future, the Unfairness Reflex will trigger a strong displaced reaction to that old wound.

Possible Sources of the Unfairness Reflex

- Siblings being compared unfairly
- Siblings being treated unequally
- Unreasonable behavioral or maturity expectations
- Competitive parents or older siblings
- Parentification of the child (When children are expected to take on adult emotional or physical responsibilities at a young age)
- Inconsistent or draconian rules or discipline
- Focus on achievement that ignores effort

Deconstructing the Unfairness Reflex

The Unfairness Reflex is an example of an old childhood wound that affects people long into their future. Not only does this reflexive reaction undermine our ability to act effectively to current challenges, but it has the potential to destroy relationships and undermine our credibility. Usually the intensity of the reaction to the current event will shock the recipient of the feeling (a relatively innocent bystander). We even might feel a little disoriented ourselves to be so enraged over something that in the long run may be unimportant. But it is the principle that has enraged us. Until we can make the unconscious reaction conscious, and understand that we are basically in a flashback, we will be stuck in this habitual reflexive response.

Steps to Healing the Unfairness Reflex

1. Observe that your reaction to the current event was exaggerated.
2. Step back, breathe deeply, and from a distance, try to identify the value or principle that has made the current event feel unfair.
3. Think about your past to identify an event or pattern of events that was similar to the current triggering experience.
4. Search for new ways to understand and take meaning from the original unfair experience. Could there be a reasonable explanation for the past behavior of the other person?

> ### Healing the Unfairness Reflex (continued)
>
> 5. Search for new ways to understand and take meaning from the original unfair experience. Could there be a reasonable explanation for the past behavior of the other person?
>
> 6. Try to imagine the event from the perspective of other people who were involved. Can you find some compassion for them and why they might have behaved as they did?
>
> 7. Breathe deeply to relax while you imagine watching the old scene from a distance, as an impartial observer noticing that the unfairness was not purposely meant to hurt you.
>
> 8. When you are able to find inner calm and distance from the old hurt, use the same process to deactivate the trigger reaction to the current event.
>
> Congratulations! Forever after this, you can notice, remember and deactivate this old wound, just by following the same steps. Becoming conscious allows you to change your unconscious reflex.

Letting Go of Old Habits

Letting go of old habits isn't as easy as it sounds. Part of the reason for this is our heart/head separation. Our hurts reside in our heart—at the level of our yearnings and feelings; the logic behind the hurt is processed in our heads. Most therapy deals with one or the other: head or heart. In order to achieve growth past pain, we must cognitively understand the reasons for the pain with possible mitigations of the circumstance and then we must also heal our heart. Our bodies register reactions to both, so paying attention to our physical reactions is the third leg of the stool. Often much of the information that drives old behaviors lies buried in our unconscious; these are often purposeful defense mechanisms, responses to traumatic emotional injuries. When the original source of the hurt is buried, we mistakenly believe that the upset is solidly based on the current event. But most of our strongest reactions are based on old triggers and hurts. And an old familiar hurt is sometimes preferable to an unknown potential hurt; so people are not so quick to let go of old habits.

Healing Old Wounds

The first step to a generic healing of old wounds is to appreciate the ways your unconscious defense mechanism protected you from intense pain. It is useful to remember that our unconscious provides a complicated resource for working out problems and pointing us in a direction that suits our highest and best purpose. Most of the time, we know what is best for us, even if we are not YET consciously choosing that practice. One of the important ways our unconscious serves us in correcting our past is by selecting values and experiences from our Family Of Origin to perpetuate in our current family. We decide both how we want to be, and how we don't want to be. As parents, we might say, "I'll never speak to my children the way my father spoke to me" or "I love the way my family went on walks together." By giving credit for the positive things we learned, and acknowledging that we have changed some of the behaviors we didn't like about our upbringing, we become aware that our unconscious defense mechanisms are working full time to steer us in an improved direction. Often, when we reject an old family behavior, we are able to heal an old hurt, by seeing progress in our own children.

Steps for Changing an Old Behavior

1. Express gratitude that the old behavior was there to help you when you needed it.
2. Accept that it will always be an option, if it is ever needed again.
3. Make a list (with at least three items on it) that might be better solutions at this time.
4. Experiment by trying the new solutions on the list.

Overcoming Family of Origin Negative Lessons

In order to overcome any old behavior, we must first understand that there are many behavior choices. Satir maintained "one choice isn't a choice at all, two choices are a dilemma, and three are the minimum necessary to be a real choice." Frequently, we don't know what other options are available. We can't technically unlearn a behavior or belief, but we can certainly challenge what we believe about it or how we behave around it. One way to change our behavior or belief is to add new information; this alone can often bring about the change we desire.

Gaining insight can also help us understand what drives us to continue a behavior. Often the old habit is associated with a positive memory, or a connection to someone no longer alive. Re-examining our assumptions about our motivation can also help us re-evaluate an old behavior.

It is important to remember that the best way to permanently change a behavior is to substitute a new, better solution. Most therapies depend upon insight and understanding to change behavior. Sometimes that is enough, but Satir stressed the importance of acknowledging the usefulness of the old coping behavior as well as adding potential new choices. By trying to just stop the old behavior, we are erasing a piece of our Self that was important at one time, and maybe still is. Naturally, our unconscious resists change; it wants to preserve good feelings about our Self and how we coped well enough to make it to the present. Remembering to be kind to ourselves, as well as to others, is an important part of nurturing growth and progress on our journey to reach health and happiness.

Worksheet for Chapter 5: Growth

Question: *Are you aware of any behaviors or life choices you've made that are consciously the opposite of what your parents would have done in those circumstances?*

Activity: *Make two lists of behaviors:*

Things I choose to do just like my parents:

1.

2.

3.

Things I choose to do the opposite way my parents did them:

1.

2.

3.

Challenge: *Allow your parents to do the things they do without feeling critical of them, and don't feel guilty about the things you choose to do differently.*

Chapter Six: Intimacy

"Intimacy is your willingness to share truth - with relevance, appropriateness, and timing."
— Virginia Satir

True intimate connection is like creating beautiful music. In fact, the translation of the Chinese symbol for a soul mate is "You sing your song and I sing mine, and they are the same." But, whether we are singing a song, or sharing a truth using a different modality of expression (e.g., touch, spoken word, art, poetry, letters, or the creations of others that express how we feel), we are taking a leap of faith to share our truest feelings and thoughts with another person. Our hope is those thoughts and feelings will be understood, appreciated, even reciprocated. This sharing of the heart is necessary to experience intimate connection.

When I talk about intimacy, I am referring to an emotional state of connection, comfort and familiarity that two people experience mutually. It always involves (as Satir said) sharing truths of the self and it is a destination that can be reached following many different paths. What is important is that both participants are interested, willing, capable and available.

Intimacy and Sex

Often when people discuss intimacy they are referring to sexual intimacy. Physical intimacy (whether it involves sex or not) can be a way of communicating, but it isn't necessarily a way that will lead to emotional intimacy. An act of sex doesn't insure there will be intimacy, just as a date doesn't necessarily lead to marriage. For many, sex is one of the many ways they express their vulnerability and commitment to their partner. For others, sex is a bodily function with no other intention or implication.

> *Pauline was thirty when she realized that her approach to dating wasn't getting her what she needed anymore. Up to then, she usually had sex on the first date with any man she fancied at her initiation. She liked to feel in charge and she'd learned that men tended to share their feelings more readily after sex. But, not having found anyone she wanted to keep around made her wonder about this approach. When she understood the sex that she'd been having wasn't really building intimacy, she began to reassess her strategy in light of a new goal: achieving intimacy.*

Physical intimacy may or may not involve sex, and emotional intimacy may not involve physical intimacy. I've worked with couples in the pornography industry whose main problem was that the physical act of sex was too mundane to allow for true emotional intimacy. In order for sex to be intimate, it must be shared in ways that communicate inner truth, connection and trust. When sex loses its connective function, it can get in the way of emotional intimacy.

Emotional intimacy reflects the closeness and connection people seek. Connection can occur regardless of gender, sex, age, culture, race, or religion and in any variety of settings. Emotional intimacy is directly related to our ability to connect with self and other. When two people share their feelings and thoughts—their truths—and feel understood and accepted for those truths, they are building intimate connection.

An important step to building or extending intimacy is to understand what intimacy means to us. These questions will help you identify what intimacy means for you.

Questions to Ask When Seeking Intimate Connection:

Why?
- Is finding intimate connection a way to enhance your life?
- Do you have a hidden agenda? A long term goal? A short term need?
- Is there an empty space you are trying to fill or fix?
- Do you attach a negative meaning about your worth to not having intimate connection? Does this meaning come from someone else? A parent? A friend?
- Do you hold a positive meaning about your worth if you have achieved an intimate connection? Does that meaning originate in your expectations about your Self?

What and How?
- What kind of intimate relationship do you seek?
- What are your short term hopes for an intimate relationship?
- What needs do you hope to fulfill by having an intimate relationship?
- What goals do you hope to achieve?
- How do you dream about intimacy being fulfilled?
- What type of setting does it involve?

Who?
- Do you care about physical features?
- Do you prefer a particular sexual orientation? Race? Marital status?
- Is the person's belief system, political affiliation, religion important to you?
- Does a potential intimate need to have particular personality traits? Extraversion? Playfulness? Flexibility?
- Do intelligence and education matter to you?

- Is job status, economic security, living standard important to you?
- Does the person need to live near you? Be willing to relocate or travel?
- Are there traits or behaviors that would rule someone out completely (e.g., egocentric, secretive, withholding, dishonest, substance abuse, bad habits, criminal record, etc.)?

When?
- Is this a reasonable time of your life to seek an intimate relationship?
- Do you have enough free time, money, and freedom to devote to finding and nurturing an intimate relationship?
- Are you ready to devote time and effort towards creating an intimate relationship?

Where?
- Are there particular places you like to spend your time (e.g., the beach, Disneyland)?
- Are you affiliated with groups based on shared interests, beliefs, ideologies or philosophies?
- Do you feel your community fits your lifestyle, core values, and beliefs?
- Do you spend time doing an activity that others might enjoy?

Given your answers to the above questions you can create a vision of the intimate relationship you desire, with the person who fits your hopes and needs.

Interested, Willing, Capable and Available

Most people don't share intimate feelings with another person unless they sense potential receptivity and reciprocity. We hope that sharing the relationship will result in something mutually satisfying for the long term. Unfortunately, some people are impaired in their ability to judge whether there is reciprocity, or how to go about identifying people who might have an interest in them. This problem can be a hard-wired disability, or it might result from lack of experience or poor modeling. Most of us endure our share of miscalculations in this area as teenagers, and learn from humbling experience when a person isn't interested. Those with Asperger Syndrome or Autism often need explicit social skills training to learn what the rest of us learn through trial and error. Most of us are lucky enough to have mentors or peers as role models or we learn from our experiences. But it is always possible to misinterpret behavior, which is why asking diplomatic questions, or moving the conversation toward what you need to know, is important.

> ### How to Judge Interest
> - Does he or she look at you (especially when you are speaking, even if it is to a group)?
> - Does he or she turn towards you, attend to what you are saying, smile at you, laugh at your jokes?
> - Does he or she address any comments or questions to you? (Does he or she listen to your response?)
> - What is the tone and content of his or her responses to you: kind, playful, flirtatious, teasing?

Beyond interest, willingness, capability and availability are essential for an intimate relationship. Assessing these generally takes time, discussion and shared experience. It may take some fairly direct conversation to assess whether a person is willing to enter into an intimate connection. There was a time when a father's first question to his daughter's potential suitor was "What are your intentions?" Unless the answer was some acceptable form of long term commitment, Dad sent him packing. While there are exceptions, most relationships aren't that straightforward anymore.

Finding out if a person is interested in the kind of intimate connection we seek can involve an investment of time and the risk of rejection. Before we can assess willingness in the other person, we need to understand our own ideas and desires for the relationships we seek. What kind of attention or time commitment do we expect or hope to receive? How exclusive do we want this relationship to be? Even in friendships there must be some agreement as to who else can be included in plans and activities. A degree of confidentiality must also be established. (e.g., Are you comfortable with this person sharing your thoughts and feelings with anyone else?)

Wouldn't it be nice if entering an intimate relationship required providing an informed consent form detailing expectations, hopes and needs? Even a marriage license doesn't provide details of this important information. [Though *1001 Questions to Ask Before You Get Married* by Leahy (2004) provides a great start for the couple that really desires full disclosure.]

Of course, we also don't know in advance if we are willing to fulfill someone else's expectations. Luckily, cavernous differences in needs and expectations usually become obvious relatively early in the relationship. When this conflict happens (usually one or the other expresses unhappiness with the way things are going), this is the time to *explicitly* discuss what each person wants and expects; if both are willing to fulfill these mutual expectations, or to compromise on some, the relationship continues.

Andrew and Amy had been dating for two weeks when Amy began to complain that they didn't see each other enough. When Andrew learned that Amy expected him to take her out to dinner at least five times per week, he realized that he didn't have the money, time, or desire to do that. They agreed to part as friends, relieved that they had discussed Amy's expectations before one of them got too attached.

We are more likely to build intimate relationships with people who share our interests, goals or background since this can significantly reduce the time it takes to feel comfortable together. When people have shared experiences, there is a greater potential that they will share similar expectations. The background or history they share often provides an immediate comfort level that may or may not be warranted. Usually, it quickly becomes clear whether or not the similar background is a basis for an ongoing connection.

Potential Shortcuts to Connection

- Common religious beliefs and practices
- Similar intellectual or political philosophies and affiliations
- Mutual friends, clubs, or social affiliation
- Similar family systems or challenges
  (e.g., birth order, sibling configuration, disabilities)
- Geographic, race, or cultural origins
  (especially if a minority in present situation)
- Similar interests, hobbies, or careers
- Shared economic, power, or social status

Even if you both share interests, backgrounds, values or hopes, there can be issues that limit your capability for intimacy. These impediments might be temporary, based on life circumstance (such as recent loss), or longstanding, such as a mood or personality disturbance (e.g., depression, narcissism or bipolar disorder). Personality traits (e.g., significant introversion), learned attitudes (e.g., pessimism, or racism) or behaviors (e.g., violence, or stonewalling) can also leave us incapable of sustaining intimate relationships. And sometimes traumatic experiences, particularly around loss and abuse, will prevent us from trusting enough to risk being close or vulnerable.

Nona and Rachel met at a meeting for Holocaust survivors. Both had been child survivors and lost most of their families. Though they never met, they both spent most of their teens in the same work camp and had survived horrific conditions. They assumed they would be great friends having such similar losses and pasts. Unfortunately, Nona was bitter about her experience. She hated Germans and non-Jews and took every opportunity to rail against them and the horrible God who had allowed this to happen to her. She'd had several unsuccessful marriages and her children didn't speak to her. Rachel, on the other hand, had blessed God for allowing her to survive and dedicated herself to helping others who had lost family. She has a large family, a loving husband and many friends whom she had included in her family over the years. It soon became clear that Nona's bitterness kept her incapable of sustaining intimate relationships, including one with Rachel.

Most of the reasons that keep us from connecting with others can be addressed in a safe therapeutic environment. Practice in trust and interpersonal risk-taking can often heal past wounds and allow people to feel trust and connection.

Individuals can be unavailable for intimate connection for several reasons. They might be in possessive relationships that have no room for any outsiders. Or they might be strongly introverted and require years to develop sufficient trust to build new intimate relationships. But most common are those who have been so wounded in the past that they have sealed off their hearts to prevent any further possibility of hurt. It is possible to help them renew hope and take another chance, but it requires patience and much love that may take a long time to be acknowledged or returned, and may never be reciprocated.

Relationship "Red Flags"

Sometimes, in the early stages of a relationship or even later, we ignore clues that could warn us that our target isn't a good candidate for intimate connection. We may hope to overcome the "Red Flags" or to rationalize and minimize the importance of what we see. Sometimes we carry the illusion that we can change people and fix their problems. Occasionally, these efforts work to sustain the intimate connection, at least temporarily. Eventually, most of us learn that the behaviors we ignored or rationalized are the reasons the relationship ends.

Ellen befriended her new neighbor, Mary. They became very close as they shared an interest in quilting and their young children were fast friends. When Mary confided that she'd stolen from her previous bank job, Ellen rationalized that Mary was young at the time. When Mary lied to her husband and was unfaithful, Ellen assumed her marriage must be unfulfilling and supported her friend by watching her sons as needed. When Mary lost her night job, Ellen hired her to work in her quilt making business. Just weeks later Ellen was only a little surprised to catch Mary lying, stealing, and secretly trying to steal her clients. She knew she had ignored Mary's pattern of dishonest behavior and she'd learned a lesson the hard way.

Paying attention to a "red flag" behavior is a form of self-protection. When someone's behavior doesn't match your values or ethics, it isn't in your best interest to ignore these clues about a person's character. This is especially true when selecting candidates for intimate relationships; similar interests are important, but like values (with words and actions that match) are most likely to result in authentic and lasting relationships. Paying attention in the early stages of sharing and learning about the other person is the best way to ensure success.

Relationship Red Flags

- Past illegal behavior
- Blaming others for all problems
- Abusive or violent behavior
- Substance use or abuse
- Condoning immoral or unethical behavior
- A history of cut-off relationships
- Holding grudges, seeking revenge
- Being secretive (hides past or current activities)
- Dishonesty, infidelity and lies
- Self-destructive or harmful behavior
- Controlling and isolating
- Hot-tempered, unwilling to discuss problems
- Few friends or no longstanding friendships

Personality Disorders

Red flags may be associated with personality disorders. Personality disorders are deeply ingrained patterns of thought and behavior that cause serious problems with interpersonal interactions. They can be difficult to spot, camouflaged by charismatic veneers. Those with Antisocial and Borderline Personality Disorders, for example, can be destructive and violent, both to themselves and to others. People with these two personality disorders tend to be intelligent, attractive, complimentary, thoughtful and charming (at least when they are befriending someone). If you have a relative with these traits, your familiarity with them may have left you accustomed to their idiosyncrasies, placing you at risk of missing the "red flags." Here are some red flags associated with personality disorders:

- A strong investment in "being right" all the time, or "never being wrong."
- Phoniness and projecting similar inauthentic motivation onto others.
- Feeling more powerful when making another feel small or embarrassed.

Be on the lookout for callousness when you expected compassion, or an unwillingness to take responsibility when something goes awry.

Intimacy, Vulnerability and Risk

Intimacy, sharing one's true inner self, requires vulnerability. When we are intimate, we are allowing the other into our private sanctum. Opening that door involves risk. Being capable of intimacy means having the strength to take the risk and knowing how to navigate that process.

Because an attempt at intimacy is not guaranteed to be successful, there is always a risk. A history of divorce or unstable past relationships can also seed doubts that any relationship can stay mutually intimate over the long term. Some people feel too hopeless to take another risk.

Risk-taking doesn't have to be accomplished with a single leap of faith. It is possible and often advisable to begin with smaller steps. Offer a part of the Self that expresses modest vulnerability. See how the other person responds. This process of building trust incrementally is the basis for increasing intimacy.

Unfortunately the response to exposed vulnerability can be unkind or defensive. This is the case when people have past negative experiences that bleed into current relationships.

Reasons People Might be Unkind in Response to Vulnerability

- They may fear ridicule or rejection—sometimes with reason.
- They may have been mocked or criticized for past disclosures or enthusiasm.
- They may have grown up with criticism and sarcasm as the norm.
- They may fear that another person's feelings will make them seem less by comparison.
- They might doubt the validity of their own feelings.

Virtually all of these scenarios are connected to past wounds that had a long-term effect upon self-worth. Those with a healthy sense of self gain pleasure in sharing another's heartfelt joy; they certainly don't feel reduced or threatened by it.

Being selective about taking risks and becoming vulnerable is a reasonable response to past experience. You probably wouldn't want an intimate connection with everyone, anyway. In fact, intimate relationships do not mean liking everyone you meet or becoming vulnerable with anyone who will have you; that would be very time consuming, and only a few people would prove worth the risk and effort.

While I believe it is wise to enter any relationship prepared and with eyes open, I don't think it is ever a waste to reach out to someone. Even when there is no response or desire to reach back, you never know what positive impact you might have made. A smile or kind word costs nothing and can have a far-reaching positive impact—risking little more than a bruised ego, yet creating infinite possibilities for positive intimate connection.

Worksheet for Chapter 6: Intimacy

Question: Do you have intimate friendships with the important people in your life?

Activity: Fill out the sociogram below by placing the names of people from your life in the circle that defines that relationship.

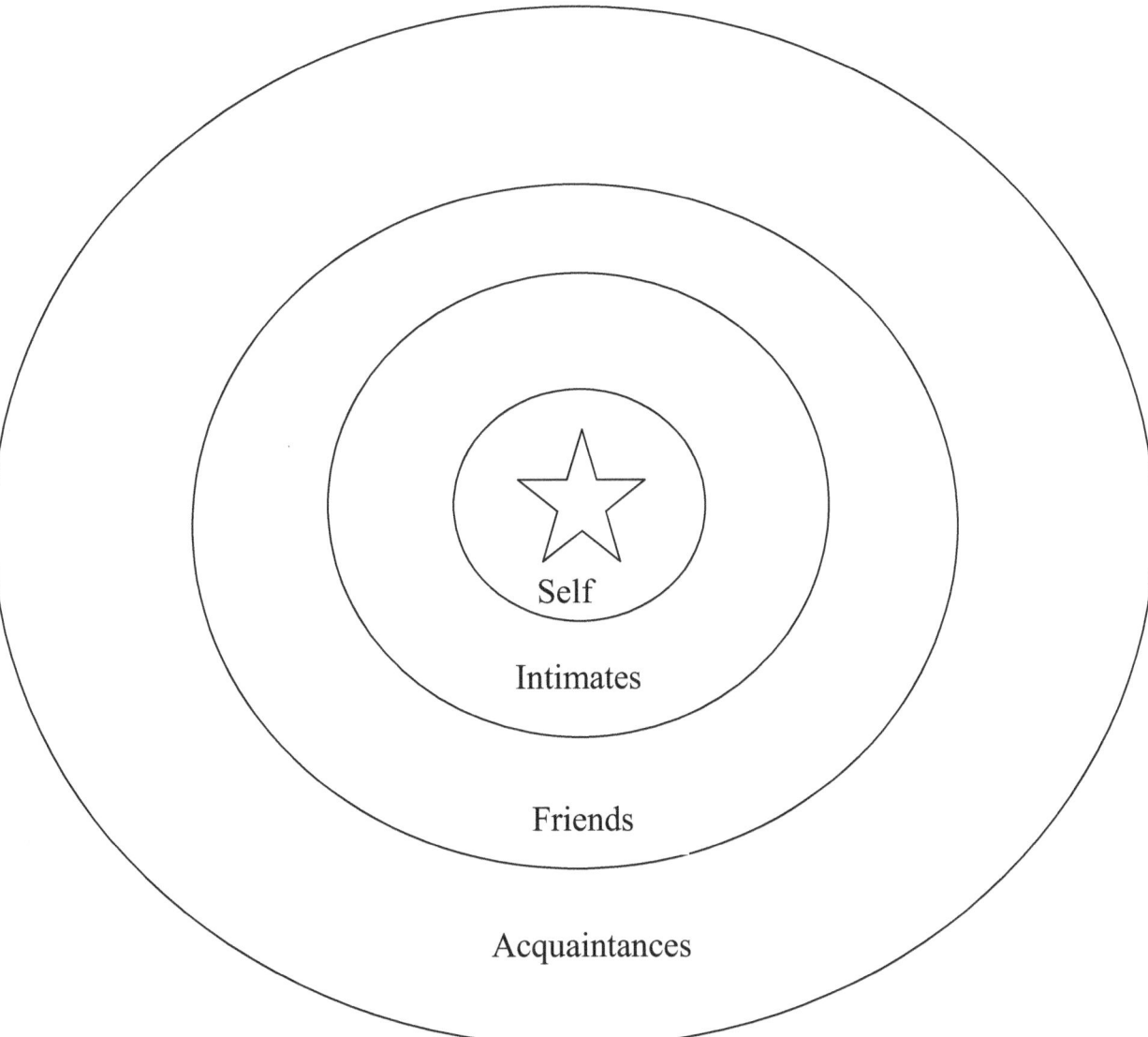

Challenge: List three actions you can take to move someone from an outside circle closer to your Self.

1)

2)

3)

Part Three: Getting to Know Your Self

"How not to be or how not to do is related to prevention; how to be or to do is related to growth."
— *Virginia Satir*

Chapter Seven: Learning Styles

"In our sameness we connect, in our differences we grow." – Virginia Satir

Different Ways of Learning

Virginia Satir was deaf during part of her early childhood. Being a bright and observant child, she watched people and analyzed their body language—how their faces looked, how their bodies moved and stood. Once her parents discovered the problem, they addressed it immediately. Still throughout her life, Virginia used her powerful observational skills to understand what people were really telling her, even if their words said something different.

When hearing is impaired, vision is often sharpened as a means of compensating. Individuals like Helen Keller, born blind and deaf, learn about the world through touch. Sight, sound and touch are windows into the world. Even when all of our senses are available to us, each of us depends more on one than the others, and develops greater strength in that preferred sense modality. Specific learning styles emerge from the combination of the dominant sense and brain hemispheric preference. This chapter is devoted to exploring the implications of learning style differences, and how self-esteem is affected by our learning style and educational experience.

Every human being experiences the world from his or her own unique perspective. Even identical Siamese twins have some separate personalities, idiosyncrasies and opinions, in spite of the fact that they share the same DNA and life experiences. From the second we take our first breath, we are using our senses to sample and collect what we need to know about life outside the womb. Once we have collected enough sensations, we use our experience and innate intelligence to categorize and sort this information until we start to see patterns, make meanings, store, retrieve and manipulate the diverse bits of knowledge we've stored somewhere in our brain as memories.

The brain is a complex information processing and control center, divided into two sides, or hemispheres: right and left. The left hemisphere is associated with the sequential, logical or linear reasoning functions of math and language—such as grammar and vocabulary. The right hemisphere is associated with more holistic reasoning functions—such as creativity, visualization, intuition, imagination. Some functions, such as emotion, are interspersed throughout both hemispheres.

The two hemispheres communicate with each other through a thick band of nerve fibers called the corpus callosum. The density of the brain and the complexity of the corpus callosum determine our capacity to process complex information. The corpus callosum is like a superhighway—the more lanes to the highway, the more cars can transit at faster speeds. While we all use both hemispheres together for many tasks, most of us lead with one hemisphere.

Just as we lead with our dominant hand, we also have a dominant sense that we prefer to use to gather information—sight (visual), hearing (auditory), or touch (tactile). We may use all our senses at different times, but some of us are more dependent upon one mode of gathering information.

The combination of hemispheric and sense modality preferences produce three major learning styles: Auditory-Sequential (ASL), Visual-Spatial (VSL) and Tactile-Kinesthetic (TKL). The sense we use most to understand the world generally corresponds with the hemispheric preference. Auditory-sequential learners have skills that are associated with the left hemisphere; visual-spatial learners are good at skills that are associated with the right hemisphere; tactile-kinesthetic learners have non-dominant balanced strengths and weaknesses associated with both hemispheres. The labels ASL/VSL/TKL are relatively self-explanatory, details are covered below.

The more intelligent the child, the more capable they are likely to be at accommodating any learning difference. However, this is like developing ambidexterity instead of using one's dominant hand. Most of the population has a definite learning style preference, and we all learn best if material is presented in our dominant style. That means listening might not be the best way for everyone to receive information, and working step-by-step might not be how they need to organize their ideas. Children are more engaged learners and feel more valued when their learning styles are accommodated.

> *In her first weeks as a preschool teacher, Shareen was fascinated at the range of interests and skills among the three-year-olds. Some spoke clearly, in short sentences, others grunted and pointed. A few children played together imaginatively creating elaborate stories with many characters; others played by themselves quietly building something or completing a puzzle. Some children, boys and girls, would choose to climb or run the whole session if they could. Even at story circle, a few children could listen to stories the whole morning, while others fell asleep or wandered off. Even at snack time, some children would carefully separate the different foods, finishing one item before tasting another; others would mash the different foods together and eat them all at once, with huge bites and noisy relish; others would take tiny bites of each food and make sure that all foods were finished at the same time. When she began teaching, Shareen thought she knew*

everything about children from her developmental psychology classes. The first day of nursery school, she realized she had a lot to learn.

For an entertaining "test" of hemispheric preference, check out the video, "Right Brain vs. Left Brain Test: Optical Illusion" (www.youtube.com/watch?v=9CEr2GfGilw). In the video a dancer twirls around. Theoretically, if you have right brain preference (VSL), she will twirl in one direction, and if you have a left brain preference (ASL), she will twirl the opposite direction. Those who learn best through touch and movement (TKL) have a totally unique experience. Try it and you'll see! It is possible to mentally change the direction of the twirler by consciously thinking about an opposite brain function, such as doing an arithmetic calculation, or imagining a movie. It may not be a scientific assessment, but it is a fun exercise.

A Tale of Three Learners

Lori, Sam and Kathy had just moved into their new apartment. Kathy looked at the massive stacks of boxes and wrapped items in various sizes and sighed, "I feel overwhelmed. Can anyone find the big wall mirror in this mess?" Lori scanned the mountain of possessions and said "Oh, there it is, leaning against the window." Sam and Kathy looked at the object Lori had indicated, then looked at each other in disbelief. Kathy sputtered, "How can you tell what it is? It looks just like everything else in here." "Wait," Sam said, "I'll find out if that is the mirror." He went to the bundle, lifted it up, and felt it through the packing layers. "Yes, it is the mirror" he confirmed, "I'll unwrap it and put it up."

Kathy is Auditory-Sequential. She would look at a stack of boxes and ascertain their contents by reading the packing list. To unpack, she probably would start with the first box marked #1 and step-by-step finish unpacking each box over time. Or, she might start with a room and unpack all the boxes that went in that room.

Sam is a Tactile-Kinesthetic Learner. He has no problem with boxes spread all over the floor. He might open them, spread out the contents and use each item as needed over time. He might just leave the boxes packed until he is forced to un-pack them out of necessity, just walking around the obstacle course until he had company.

Lori is a Visual-Spatial Learner. She can look at a mass of boxes and scan them for differences, quickly identifying the shape of the wrapped item and mentally comparing it to the picture in her mind of what the item looked like before it was wrapped. She is likely to want to unpack, sort, and put everything away as soon as possible because it annoys her to bump into boxes and have her visual field too messy.

Learning Style Affects Every Part of Your Life

Auditory-Sequential, Visual-Spatial, and Tactile-Kinesthetic describe both modes of input and methods of organization. The first word in the pair refers to how information is best absorbed for understanding and retention. The second describes how information is best stored or organized in memory. A variety of factors facilitates or impedes our ability to process the world around us: innate intelligence, personality, interpersonal influences, temperament, perception, motor skills, resources, and, particularly, learning style affect the way we learn and apply what we experience.

> *Elizabeth complained that she could not put together the cabinet even though she had the instructions, and had attempted to follow them to the letter. Megan looked at the cabinet pieces spread out before her friend and said, "Let me help, I love doing this stuff." Minutes later, without even looking at the instructions, Megan had the cabinet assembled. Elizabeth was an auditory-sequential learner, and it wouldn't have occurred to her **not** to follow instructions step-by-step. Megan is a visual-spatial learner who looks at the whole and has an intuitive understanding of how the pieces fit together.*

Auditory-Sequential Learners (ASLs)

Our left hemispheres are important for communication and time management. They allow us to attend to details, make judgments, set priorities, meet deadlines and function well in school. Auditory-sequential skills are essential in an environment where employees must follow step-by-step verbal instructions, where writing must be concise and clear, and in a hierarchical system (business, education, politics, etc.). Those who have an auditory-sequential learning style fit in well with societal expectations.

Auditory Sequential Learners

- understand oral directions and explanations.
- learn step-by-step, adding to their knowledge base in a sequence.
- gain satisfaction from mastering easy material and progressing in difficulty.
- learn by trial and error, incrementally getting to the correct combination.
- are likely be timely and can estimate how long things will take.
- have good short-term memory; repetition aids in long-term retention.
- learn to read phonetically.
- have no difficulty with spelling.
- are good at arithmetic, and can explain the steps to getting an answer.

Visual-Spatial Learners (VSLs)

Our right hemispheres are visual rather than verbal. Those with a right-hemispheric preference—visual-spatial learners—are more adept with space than with time. While they communicate in words, verbal communication is more like a second language. As with speaking a second language, translation takes time and brain power, and some people never learn to do it proficiently. Reading, writing and spelling are more difficult for VSLs to master. As big-picture-thinkers, they are hardwired to see patterns and relationships. They are more likely to succeed with calculus and physics than with memorizing their math facts. They understand the whole and may miss the details. Visual-spatial skills are essential for architects, surgeons, pilots, designers, mathematicians, scientists, and graphic artists. They are becoming more prized in the 21st century as the world shifts from the Computer Data Age to the Networked Information Age.

Visual-Spatial Learners

- think and remember things in pictures or movies.
- learn by watching a demonstration or illustration.
- are good at scanning and uncovering hidden objects and meanings.
- are creative and think of original solutions to problems.
- like to see the whole picture before zeroing in on the parts.
- can mentally imagine spatial changes and movement.
- are good synthesizers, pattern seekers, and inventors.
- know solutions intuitively, have difficulty showing steps.

Is it possible for a speaker to bridge the gap between different types of learners and keep a mixed learning style audience fully engaged? There are a few dynamic speakers who manage to do this. One of these is Jean Houston, scholar, philosopher, lecturer, and social activist.

So how does Houston connect to listeners who don't usually enjoy listening? For one thing, she uses words to paint a vivid picture, as she makes her point. Story telling is an art; it must combine content, context, structure, pacing, tone, and character development by using the voice and body to create a dance that moves the observer. A well told story must activate and enlist the imagination, as well as impart facts and ideas; in this Houston excels.

Houston understands how to build suspense, inspire emotion and maintain rapt attention. She uses drama to weave a basis for identification—describing picturesque details, employing compelling metaphors, similes and comparisons; in the end, she has composed a symphony of words to touch, move and inspire her audience to think and act. Houston offers us her open heart and authenticity to help us *care about her and her subject. By the end of her presentation; we feel that we know **her**, as well as the subject she presents.*

Tactile-Kinesthetic Learners (TKLs)

Because they are focused on their physical needs and like to move regularly, TKLs are especially at odds with a traditional teaching environment that expects them to sit and listen for long periods of time. Of the three learning styles, TKLs are most likely to get into trouble, be diagnosed with attention deficit disorder, and be given medication to control their behavior. They can be challenging as toddlers because they focus on building physical skills before verbal ones, and they may use physical solutions (like biting or hitting) to solve problems. They touch things, take them apart, and go places that may dismay even the most relaxed parent. Luckily, they also tend to have faster reflexes and know their physical limitations better than children with other learning styles. They excel in areas which allow them movement; they are counted among our athletes, dancers, police force, fire department, military, mechanics, Emergency Room doctors and nurses, and construction workers.

Tactile-Kinesthetic Learners

- learn by touching and manipulating objects.
- learn by personal experience of trial and error, over time.
- are good at doing things, especially physical activities.
- are sensitive to their physical environment and comfort.
- like to spread their belongings out, touch them.
- need to move, like to make noise (but not hear it).
- are absorbed in the present, lose track of time.

Twyla Tharp is a gifted dancer and choreographer. Her mother once described taking the young Twyla to a psychiatrist to be given medication for her ADHD. He questioned her briefly, then asked her to wait in his office/playroom while he and her mother were in the next room. For an hour they watched Twyla through a one-way mirror as she danced and entertained herself creating dance routines to entertain herself. The psychiatrist concluded, "Twyla Tharp does not have ADHD. Ms. Tharp is a dancer and should be excused from tasks that do not accommodate her creative movement."

Schools Tend to Teach to the Auditory Sequential Learner

A lot has been written for educators about various kinds of intelligences and learning styles. People excel in different areas using different modalities to understand their world. We need only look at families to see that members often demonstrate completely different areas of expertise, skills, interests and learning styles. The understanding and incorporation of learning styles into mainstream education is still in its early stages. Schools sometimes apply this information inappropriately. They may adopt a new teaching method and then force everyone to switch to the "new way," ignoring the fact that the old method worked perfectly for some of the children.

The educational model generally still used today was created in the image of early industrialization—creating workers with uniform skills who would conform, and have a high tolerance for boring, repetitive tasks. In the past, these skills were needed to fill production lines and the jobs that made factories profitable. Education of the masses—sitting quietly, doing their jobs robotically, working sequentially on worksheets in timed intervals—was a microcosm of what they were expected to do in the workplace, i.e. a factory.

The predecessor of mass education was similar. Historically, teachers lectured and students sat quietly at their desks. Students were taught in an auditory-sequential manner—and they were expected to gain the information they needed by listening (auditory) to step-by-step (sequential) instructions. The extension of education from an elite privilege to a democratic popular right unwittingly promulgated the ASL model through mass production. Education of the masses became a macrocosm of the factory.

The education system rewarded people who excelled in ASL skills. High achieving ASL students (who hold positive associations with their school experience) are also likely to become teachers. The ASL teachers then employ ASL teaching strategies and the cycle repeats. This makes school highly accessible for ASLs, but a challenge for others. There appear to be increasing numbers of children who do not learn as ASLs and find themselves lost and confused. Research conducted at the Gifted Development Center suggests that only one-third of today's students actually show an ASL preference, while two-thirds prefer VSL teaching methods. (See *Upside-Down Brilliance: The Visual-Spatial Learner* by Linda Silverman for more information.)

Hopefully, the impulse to accommodate learning styles in education will progress similarly to overcoming sexism. Originally, only boys were educated. When education was expanded to include girls, the curriculum for girls was quite different. They were often sent to finishing schools, where they were taught how to manage a home. Beliefs that girls should be educated to be good homemakers continued into the 1960s, when girls were required to take cooking, sewing, and homemaking classes, while boys took print shop, machine shop and auto mechanics. All girls were counseled to take typing classes, on the off chance that they couldn't land a husband and would end up as a secretary. As late as the 1980s, even in a relatively young and hip business like the music industry, most executives (the majority men), did not know how to touch type, and depended upon secretaries to compose and produce their written correspondence. It is only in the last few decades that women were expected to plan for a career other than raising children and maintaining their husband's life style.

> *In 1968, Carla's science teacher took her aside and praised her exceptional achievements in the electricity unit the class had been studying. The teacher was in awe of her innate understanding of circuitry and how things worked. "Carla!" she exclaimed," You should become a science teacher." Carla became a teacher, but she encourages her stellar students, of either sex, to become electrical engineers and has them inventing things instead of writing reports.*

Educating to individual differences is compromised by one-size-fits-all philosophies, simplistic governmental mandates, budget cuts, and the emphasis on test scores. The trend of the last few decades has been for government to mandate more, not less, of the school day. The more administration and governments limit what and how teachers can teach, the less likely it is that learning styles will be taken into account and that students who are not ASLs will get their needs met. Funding cuts and shrinking enrollment have further eroded the quality and breadth of instruction. School districts cut arts, vocational training, and cultural literacy programs, essentially leaving a curriculum taught using auditory-sequential teaching techniques.

Learning Style Points to Remember

- Most people demonstrate some of the characteristics of all three learning styles.
- A significant percentage of the population has a strong preference for a particular learning style.
- When forced to use a non-dominant learning style, we may not learn as well or as quickly, and may get fatigued, using behavior that distracts or recovers our attention.
- ASLs trust what they hear, and prefer oral interactions—explanations, directions, instruction, and discussion.
- VSLs trust what they observe—behavior, body language, illustrations, diagrams, and modeling make the greatest impact on them.
- TKLs learn and communicate through touch and movement—allowing them to move helps them hear and remember more efficiently. Spoken rhymes with gesture and active exercises provide a pathway for interaction and retention.
- Most people demonstrate some of the characteristics of all three learning styles.

Tom and Lottie were expelled from a public high school for truancy, disruptive behavior and failing classes. They were transferred to a high school for "problem students." At the new school Tommy, a TKL, was allowed to sprawl on a bean bag chair during lectures, and to create power point presentations and 3D computer models to demonstrate that he'd learned the material. Lottie, a VSL, became the "class illustrator." She delighted in making graphic drawings of class lectures then posting them on the school website for others to use. Both graduated from the school with honors. After graduation, Lottie was hired as a graphic illustrator for business meetings. Tom went on to college in computer technology and eventually began to work for a company that specialized in computer-generated special effects in movies.

> **Applying Information on Learning Style Differences**
>
> Once you understand your particular style (or that of those with whom you work and live) and how it impacts life experience, you can:
>
> - Use the tricks, tools and techniques that are available for your particular style (check the website www.VisualSpatial.org).
>
> - Notice if learning challenges are related to the teaching style. Try recording a lecture and replay it while doing something that helps with information retention:
>   TKLs: exercise while you listen;
>   VSLs: doodle or create a cartoon about the information.
>
> - Look for other ways to access information that matches your learning style:
>   TKLs: attend a participatory simulation or live demonstration;
>   VSLs: rent a video or find an illustrated version of the book.
>
> - Educate your teachers and administrators about learning style differences and how to teach in different ways.
>
> - Select a career that optimizes your learning style and skills:
>   TKLs: incorporate movement and variety;
>   VSLs: be creative and notice the environment.

Knowing and accommodating learning styles can mean the difference between frustration and failure, and the successful fulfillment of our goals and dreams. Gaining acceptance for the impact of learning styles will take time and tenacity.

Worksheet for Chapter 7: Learning Styles

Question: *What is your dominant learning style? Can you think of times it would have helped to know this?*

Activity: *Considering the traits of your dominant learning style, list three areas in which that trait has been helpful to you. List three areas where that trait has been a disadvantage.*

My learning style has been really helpful to me in:

    a)

    b)

    c)

My learning style has been a disadvantage to me in:

    a)

    b)

    c)

Challenge: *Can you turn the disadvantages into advantages through creative problem solving for the future?*

Chapter Eight: Personality

"Feelings of worth can flourish only in an atmosphere where individual differences are appreciated, mistakes are tolerated, communication is open, and rules are flexible - the kind of atmosphere that is found in a nurturing family."   – *Virginia Satir*

Virginia Satir described human behavior using the metaphor of an iceberg. We only see a part of it above the waterline, the "tip of the iceberg." The majority of the iceberg floats below the water, often causing problems for those who misjudge how much of it is hidden. (See illustration at start of Chapter 14.)

The tip of the iceberg represents the behavior the rest of the world can see and hear. It includes our overt behaviors, acts or words that others experience, and as we near the waterline, our defenses and coping mechanisms. Submerged below the water, in our internal personal realm, are the invisible but very real motivators that determine what we present to the world and how we present it. These driving elements include: our feelings (happy, sad, angry etc.); our feeling about our feelings (mediated by the rules we've learned about what feelings are acceptable); our perceptions (what we sense, the meanings we attribute to what we sense, the beliefs, thoughts and values we ascribe to those meanings); our expectations (what we think **should** happen); and our yearnings (what we **hope** will happen). All of these are integrated in our sense of Self which fluctuates depending upon current circumstances and lifelong experiences. Much of this very active process occurs below our own consciousness, and very rapidly. No wonder human behavior can be confusing!

Most of us do not enjoy feeling confused. Below the water is the process we use to make sense out of the world stimulating our senses. We look for patterns and assign meanings (not always accurate) to our perceptions (also not necessarily the whole story). Our subsequent feelings may then be based on incorrect meanings. Based upon our expectations, internal rules, yearnings and longings, these incorrect meanings can not only distance us from others, but can also undermine our sense of Self.

> *Pam gave her friend Janet a gift with a beautiful handmade card. Janet asked if Pam had made "it," referring to the card. Pam yearned for Janet's approval and had expected to be thanked profusely. When Pam received a question instead of praise, her immediate disappointment degenerated into a feeling of disapproval about the gift in general. She created the meaning that Janet didn't like her gift and was wondering if she could return "it," the gift. She felt disappointed and hurt, which lowered her self-esteem and confidence. To defend her sense of Self, she angrily responded that Janet should just return the gift to the store, and this*

was the last gift she would ever give her. Janet, completely confused by Pam's reaction, began to reevaluate whether she wanted to be friends with this irrational person. Had Pam just answered the question, that she had made the gift card and bought the gift, she could have saved herself and Janet a lot of grief.

The main purpose of the meaning-making process is to be able to predict behavior so we can feel confident going out into world without being hurt. We blindly choose to think our perceptions (the information that comes from our senses) are accurate pieces of a larger puzzle. We search them for patterns and assign meanings to them in an attempt to protect our sense of Self. Alas, perceptions are colored not only by beliefs, assumptions, focus, fears, and hopes, but also by personality type.

This chapter addresses the role of personality type in understanding the world. This knowledge can create better access to compassion and connection. Carl Gustav Jung (1875-1961) was a pioneering Swiss psychiatrist who founded Analytical Psychology. He comprehensively studied one version of dream analysis, and defined four life functions that are each affected by a particular area of personality difference. In his 1923 book, *Psychological Types,* Jung defined personality groupings of these differences as archetypes that present a universal model of a person, personality and behavior. Jung's types were later codified in the *Myers-Briggs Type Indicator* (Myers, 1962).

Myers-Briggs' Personality Difference Areas
(and Jungian Life Functions)

- **Extroversion vs. Introversion**
  How people affect our energy

- **Sensing vs. Intuitive**
  How we get our information

- **Thinking vs. Feeling**
  How we process the received information

- **Judging vs. Perceiving**
  How we organize our lives

Personality type significantly impacts how we perceive the world. Misperceptions flowing from differences in personality might easily be the single most common source of conflict in relationships. No matter what social system—home, school, work—our personality type carries implications about behavior, feelings, and relationships.

Understanding Personality Differences

If we don't understand potential common sources of personality conflict, we are susceptible to using our "meaning making" to make incorrect assumptions about intention and purpose. It is essential to know our own personality type so that we can create an environment that allows us to be comfortable and minimizes conflict. Without this larger framework we are condemned to interpret conflict as others' short sighted mistakes. Accepting the innate impact of personality on perception on both sides and looking back through the window of the other's perspective allows us to defuse conflicts and see them less as misunderstandings and more as simple differences in perception.

Much of our personality is hard-wired at birth. Since 1979, Bouchard and his colleagues (1990) at the University of Minnesota followed more than 350 pairs of twins, including 44 pairs of identical twins who were raised apart (meeting for the first time in the course of the study). For most of the traits measured, more than half the variation in personality was found to be due to heredity, leaving less than half determined by the influence of parents, home environment and other experiences in life. This makes understanding personality differences, even in young children, an important consideration when raising them. It also means that hoping to "change" or "train" people to react differently requires careful reconsideration.

Katya's family worried that she was shy and withdrawn. Even as a baby she would cling to her parents and cry in unfamiliar settings. For years, any suggestion that she needed to meet new people or join large organizations threw her into a panic. She tearfully described the nightmare of her parents' always pushing her to be more outgoing. As an adult, Katya's personality test revealed and normalized her introverted personality type. Once she could shed her shame at being the only introvert in a family of extroverts, she could embrace her natural personality; she found the one good friend she needed, created a safe, familiar environment, and accommodated her needs. Unlike the hermit her parents feared she would become, once she balanced social time (which drained her), with alone time (to recharge her energy); she could happily participate in both activities without anxiety.

Personality preferences can be observed in infants. One baby is easy to distract and redirect when upset, while another will tenaciously reject the same distraction; one baby is easily startled, the next unflappable; one enjoys attention and crowds; another withdraws when someone comes near. Some babies are cuddly and enjoy being held and handled, others stiffen when touched. These early preferences differentiate individuals throughout their development. Some children crave playmates, while others prefer to be alone. Some children understand things intuitively; others need concrete proof to believe an assertion. Timeliness, anxiety levels, risk tolerance, decisiveness and need for company all relate to personality type differences.

Personality typology was studied by philosophers as far back as ancient Greece. Hippocrates in his "Nature of Man" described a theory of personality he called Humoralism. Hippocrates used existing medical knowledge, logic and careful observation to suggest four bodily fluids or humors were at the root of all the major questions of disease, health and personality.

Human beings are vulnerable and dependent for much of their first decade of life. It is crucial to their sense of well-being that their caretakers understand their personality needs. Even when they become independent, their ability to predict when people (starting with parents and siblings) will behave as "friend or foe" can determine immediate safety, health and welfare.

> *Josie described her childhood as "precarious." Angry, alcoholic parents and violent older siblings meant that Josie had to be hyper-vigilant to avoid being physically and emotionally harmed. She became a keen observer of environmental stressors and dangerous situations. From a mile away, Josie could spot "difficult" personalities, and people who had reached their limit. This life skill proved essential when she decided to enter a career in law enforcement.*

Instruments have been developed to identify, simplify and explain personality and behavior. These instruments have proven useful in a wide range of settings and in a variety of decision points such as educational, career and marital selection—not to mention proving invaluable to maintaining satisfying relationships.

With enough knowledge of personality, experience and temperament, human beings are surprisingly predictable. When activated, we all have the same instinctive choices for spontaneous protection: fight, flight or hide. How these choices are made and which we select in a given situation is influenced by our personality type, and the complicated calculations we spontaneously make when feeling threatened. The strength of the personality trait, the beliefs and expectations of others (e.g. parent, teacher, community, co-worker or spouse) will influence how that trait will manifest in behavior. Knowing our personality profile allows us to understand our own motivations and needs, so we can choose to create a life that fulfills us.

Discovering Your Personality Type

While there are many tools for defining personality types, the most common and well researched is the *Myers-Briggs Type Indicator* (MBTI) originally developed by Isabelle Briggs Myers and her mother, Katharine Cook Briggs during World War II. Its purpose was to help people understand each other and avoid destructive conflicts (Myers, I.B. with Myers, P.B., 1980). Based on Jung's theories, the original questionnaire was expanded and published in 1962 as the *Myers-Briggs Type Indicator* (MBTI). Unlike many personality inventories, it focuses on normal populations and distinguishes between naturally occurring differences without assessing a value hierarchy. It yields sixteen personality type combinations (four categories, two extremes in each category). None is better than another. Certain types are more suited to specific career choices or to roles within an organization.

There are many websites that offer online administration of the MBTI with or without a full explanatory report of the results. Many marriage and family therapists and psychologists are also trained in administering and scoring the instrument. Additionally, life and career counselors often offer it as part of their services. Because it is a forced choice test of preferences, the validity of the responses is dependent upon truthfulness as well as not "over-thinking" the simple comparisons. For those whose personalities are not decidedly on one side of the continuum or the other, every answer would be "it depends on..." followed by a myriad of options under different circumstances. Sometimes it helps to imagine, "How would I have responded before I became socialized to fulfill others' expectations of me?" There are no wrong answers, and no typology is innately superior to another, even though we often value the traits in our own typology above those with our opposite type.

Factors that Can Influence the Validity of Results on the MBTI

Family rules	Mental health
Cultural values	Beliefs and prejudices
Typology of parents	Reasons for taking the MBTI
Who will see the results	Anxiety
Self-awareness	Administrative setting
Privacy needs	Strong public persona

Once you have a typology for yourself (the four letters that represent your score) you need only Google the letter combination to get a plethora of information and feedback. Some of the web explanations sound more like astrology than science, but the MBTI assessment has been validated on millions of people. A shorter, self-scoring adaptation of the MBTI, the *Kiersey Temperament Sorter*, was developed and published in the 1978 book by David Kiersey and Marilyn Bates, *Please Understand Me*. This test is available for free, on line at: www.Keirsey.com. Both tests provide valuable insight into how people experience, organize, and make decisions.

In the MBTI and Kiersey Temperament Sorter, each dimension is presented in a pair of contrasting traits, and defines a different aspect of personality on a continuum. Most people display a mix of both traits, others display some traits in a particular context, and some are most comfortable at an extreme end of the continuum. If a large discrepancy occurs between people in a significant relationship, it can cause conflict and discord—the larger the discrepancy in scores, the more difficult it is to understand, accept and accommodate the other. However, just understanding that these large differences exist can relieve some of the emotional response to the resulting conflicts.

> *Candice and Tom fell madly in love upon their first meeting. They "completed" each other, providing perfect answers to lifelong personality questions. Where Candice (an ENFP) was gregarious, enthusiastic, spontaneous and intuitive, Tom was grounded, thoughtful, practical, reliable, logical and dependable. They married and had a child. Conflicts began when Tom began to see Candice's spontaneity and enthusiasm as unfocused and flaky. Tom's dependability began to feel boring and predictable; it seemed to constrain Candice's pleasure in seeking surprises and living in the moment. They both began to feel the other was purposely trying to annoy and undermine them. Once they understood that the same traits that had brought them together were pushing them apart, they could stop personalizing the differences, and begin to seek compromises.*

The following sections explore the four personality type dimensions.

Introversion-Extroversion

The Introversion/Extroversion dimension describes the way we respond to social interactions (gaining or drained of energy) and where we process information or make decisions (internally or externally). Commonly, the words *introvert* and *extravert* are used to describe how people act in groups: quiet or gregarious. The original Jungian terms had a different meaning, not necessarily correlated with public behavior. The Jungian distinction focuses on how the experience affects one's energy level after the public performance. In the Jungian sense, introverted types can still be quite extroverted in public settings.

Introverted types have an active internal life—weighing options, surveying preferences, making plans, decisions, and experiencing feelings internally in a private way. When they choose to share what they have been working on, it is usually a finished product. They may need time to recharge after being with people (the more people, the more energy expended) or before discussing conflicts.

Extroverted types gain energy from interacting with others. They are often energized after a social event. They enjoy making decisions with others, getting input, discussing ideas and dreams well before any decision has been made. They want resolution of conflict immediately.

Traits of Introversion/Extroversion (I/E) Dimension

An Introverted Type:	**An Extroverted Type:**
Gets tired after socializing	Is energized by socializing
Thinks about things, ideas	Talks about things, ideas with everyone
Makes own decisions	Solicits input from others for decisions
Prefers to work alone on projects	Prefers to work on group projects
Enjoys working alone without conversation	Prefers working with others, discussing work
Needs time to recharge after school or work	Likes going directly from school or work to more activities
Is concerned with privacy, keeps confidences	Likes to share information and personal truths
Likes to control and limit attendance at events	Enjoys large events: "the more, the merrier"
Avoids being the center of attention	Enjoys attention and wants credit for efforts
Needs to withdraw in the face of strong feelings	Prefers to discuss conflict immediately to full resolution
Presents ideas after full consideration, avoids considering possibilities, explaining thought process	Presents ideas while soliciting discussion about them

Sensing-Intuitive

The Sensing/iNtuitive (abbreviated S/N) continuum refers to how we gather information, and what kind of information we trust in forming opinions and making decisions. Sensing types trust what they experience through their senses—what they can see and hear and touch; when they gather information they will seek out concrete references (weighing their credibility), and "proof," such as statistics and scientific measures. iNtuitive types trust their intuition and often cannot explain how they know what they know to someone else. Given the choice between a set of facts or a "gut feeling," sensing types will select the "facts;" iNtuitive types will feel more confident "going with their gut."

Traits of the Sensing/iNtuitive (S/N) Dimension

A Sensing Type:	**An Intuitive Type:**
Trusts personal physical experiences	Trusts inner knowing
Concrete	Abstract
Observant	Lives in world of ideas
Practical	Idealistic
Believes in a reliable, shared reality	Believes we all have a unique, valid worldview
Comfortable with the known	Imaginative, inventive, loves possibilities
Likes facts and verifiable information	Prefers metaphor and indirect knowledge
Can miss or discount information if it doesn't fit his or her past experience or knowledge	Can entertain ideas that do not fit current beliefs or accepted paradigm
Can prove his or her assertions	Resents having to prove conclusions (and may not be able to prove them)

Thinking-Feeling

The Thinking/Feeling dimension describes how we process information and make decisions. Most people use a combination of both, but if there is a conflict between thought and feeling, most people will favor one over the other in the final decision.

Thinking types prefer to analyze all available information necessary to make a decision. They will use logic and practical calculations to decide the best possible course of action.

Feeling types prefers to follow their heart, even if it isn't the wisest or most logical and practical choice. They tend to be very sensitive to the feelings and opinions of others, and can be quite dramatic in their need to follow their heart.

Traits of the Thinking/Feeling (T/F) Dimension

A Thinking Type:	A Feeling Type:
Analyzes facts using logic	Makes decisions using feelings
Compares and weighs practical considerations making decisions	Factors the feelings, needs and when wishes of others in decisions
Trusts systematic evaluation of statistics	Trusts the heart as a guide to the best choice
Likes reasonable justification for making one decision instead of another	Doesn't need to justify a decision with "reason" as long as it has "heart reasons"
Prefers to be right rather than tactful	Protects other people's feelings at the expense of truth

Judging-Perceiving

The Judging/Perceiving dimension defines the process used to organize the practical aspects of life, such as schedules, commitments, timeliness, and fulfilling responsibilities. The extremes of this category present significant implications for group processes, team cohesiveness, marital harmony, educational achievement and even job satisfaction.

> *A priest once told me that he required all marital candidates to take the MBTI. He explained that in his many years of performing marriages, he'd found that couples at the extreme opposite ends of the Judging/Perceiving continuum faced overwhelming obstacles to achieving a happy long-term marriage. He would not perform nuptials likely to fail from the start.*

In this context, Judging refers to using judgment, as in making decisions (as opposed to the common meaning of "judgmental"). Judging types value closure, organization, plans, timeliness, strategies, commitment, decisiveness, and a clearly defined hierarchy with rules and consequences. Once they have made a decision, they do not enjoy changes.

Perceiving types enjoy and value process, collaboration, consensus decision-making, flexibility, unscheduled time, options, spontaneity, change, and have a high tolerance for ambiguity.

Traits of the Judging/Perceiving (J/P) Dimension

A Judging Type:	A Perceiving Type:
Prefers closure	Likes to keep options open
Acts decisively	Is comfortable with ambiguity
Creates a plan for each day	Likes unscheduled time to relax
Prefers advance notice	Enjoys surprises and values serendipity
Sticks to the plan	Makes adjustments to plans
Is on time or early to appointment	Is often relaxed about appointment times, considering them approximations
Begins tasks as soon as they are assigned; completes them long before they are due	Is not motivated by deadlines and completes tasks at the last minute
Is dependable	Is flexible
Keeps promises and agreements at all costs	Adjusts agreements situationally
Follows a rule to the letter	Fulfills the spirit of a rule's intention; sees rules as guidelines
Prefers to maintain traditions and rituals	Likes to make new traditions to fit circumstances
Completes tasks systematically	Completes tasks creatively
Manages employee progress closely	Encourages autonomy in employees
Anticipates and proactively avoids problems	Puts out fires as they arise
Notices and suggests ways to help others improve performance and productivity	Acknowledges and rewards performance and productivity
Maintains detailed calendars and "to do" lists	Knows when what is scheduled needs to be done
Completes responsibilities quickly	Hyper-focuses on performing tasks well spends extra time, even if late
Maintains a clean, well-organized workspace	May spread work over large area and leave in place until completed
Completes one task before starting the next	May work on several projects at the same time with various stages of completion

Jerry described his first job with a company that hadn't turned a profit in 4 years, partly because they suffered from an employee turnover rate triple the national average. The CEO asked all employees to take a MBTI with the option of moving to a job that better fit their personality typology. Not even a year after the massive job reassignment, the company became profitable, and morale improved ten-fold. Jerry credited his later success to that experience.

Points to Remember about Personality Type

All types are necessary in life because they bring different necessary skill sets to an effort—*"a baseball team full of shortstops wouldn't win very many games."*

- Strong differences between people or in families can be bridged if there is respect for and acceptance of the difference, and acknowledgement of the blessings of that type—*"We can always count on Joan to get us there on time." "Johnny makes everything more fun."*

- People are often drawn to different personality types because they fill in a gap in their own personality—*"I married my husband because he was solid as a rock; I divorced him because he was cold as a stone."*

- It is easy to fall into a blaming stance when there are personality type differences. All types have both positive and negative implications, and most systems need aspects of all types at different times in different roles—*"If everyone were king, nothing would get done."*

- When there is likely to be a conflict between types, the best strategy is to anticipate the stressor to negotiate a mutually satisfying solution—*"The plane leaves in two hours; let's drive separately so you can take your time packing and I won't feel anxious about missing the plane."*

Worksheet for Chapter 8: Personality

Question: *In what ways has your personality type affected your life and relationships?*

Activity: *For each type dimension, list one challenge you've had to face because of your type. (e.g. Introversion- Have avoided social events)*

Introversion-Extroversion

Sensing-Intuitive

Thinking-Feeling

Judging-Perceiving

Challenge: *Can you think of a compromise behavior that would allow you to overcome the challenges above while still honoring your personality type?*

Chapter Nine: Core Values

"Just as a yearning is a universal need for something and a longing is a person-specific need, groups may have value systems, but Core Values (while often shared with many people) are defined by individuals for themselves" — *Virginia Satir*

A Core Value is a deeply held principle that one identifies with so strongly that it feels like it defines one's essence; it affects all aspects of one's life. These values are reflections of deep inner feelings. We all have Core Values, whether we are consciously aware of them or not. They are bedrock beliefs that form the foundations of our feelings and actions. We know many of them because they help us set goals (like New Year's resolutions) and stop us from doing things we will later regret. Others may live in our unconscious. They still guide our behavior, life choices, personal relationships, and business practices. They usually define what we teach others, what makes us proud and what keeps us motivated. Core Values are powerful.

> *On her third birthday, Amy announced that she needed to become a vegan because she could not bear the thought of eating something that had once had feelings. At 58, Tom was a virtual recluse. He didn't like people. He spent all his spare time working in a rescue center for abused dogs. Jenna, age 12, was incensed that her mother had "ruined her life" by telling her father that she had gotten her period. Richard asked for a divorce when he discovered his new wife had lied to him about her past.*

All of these people were acting in integrity with their Core Values: Amy valued all life; Tom believed in animal rights; Jenna valued her privacy and maintaining a confidence; and Richard's deepest Core Value was truthfulness.

Unconscious Core Values can trigger strong emotions, both positive and negative. Often, when we have a disproportionate reaction to an event, a Core Value has been violated. The event itself or the perception of what happened can hide the real reason for the reaction. The true source of the pain is our disappointment over the Core Value violation.

> *James came into my office seething because of a recent experience with his friend, Joe. James had called Joe to vent about something upsetting him when Joe interrupted the narrative with "Whoa, James, could you watch the swearing? I'm driving, the cell phone is on speaker; my little girl is hearing all this." James became even more upset, responded "F-- you" and hung up.*

When I spoke with him, he still carried the rage of the event. We explored what had triggered his anger, and he realized that it was the phone being on speaker (Core Value: privacy) without his permission (Core Value: respect or control). We also identified anger over the fact that he had been chastised for something he didn't know he wasn't supposed to do (Core Value: fairness or trying to please but being misunderstood); and that Joe proved he wasn't listening to what James was saying when he focused on his language (Core Value: being acknowledged and seen). Additionally, James identified a strong need to be accepted without judgment (Core Value: acceptance), so being chastised for his behavior violated that value, as well. While James admitted he valued all the above, in this case, it was his Core Value of privacy and respect that had triggered the huge response. Once he knew that, he started to calm down.

James admitted that Joe was kind in the way he asked for his needs to be met, and that Joe had a right to protect his daughter, and perhaps his state required hands-free cell phone use while driving. James also admitted that the relationship was worth repairing. Once the basis for the reaction was revealed and James could accept that Joe hadn't intentionally violated his own Core Values, his anger dissolved. James was then freed to admit that he should apologize for his reaction and that he could explain to Joe about being sensitive to others overhearing his conversation. He practiced asking Joe to tell him if the phone was on speaker or if they couldn't talk privately.

After letting go of his rage, James could begin to understand how he had experienced these violations many times in the past (which had built up heightened sensitivity and reaction) and how he could recognize and handle those experiences more positively in the future.

Defusing Disproportionate Rage (for Yourself)

Step One: Draw or write a story board or list of "what happened" moment by moment.
  A. I called Joe to vent. I started to tell Joe the story in my own words.
  B. Joe stopped me saying, *"Whoa, James, could you watch the swearing? I'm driving and the cell phone is on speaker; my little girl is hearing all this."*
  C. I became enraged.
  D. I screamed "F-you."
  E. I hung up on Joe.

Step Two: After each item, add the Core Value that had been violated.
  A. I called Joe to vent. I started to tell Joe the story in my own words.
  B. Joe stopped me, saying, *"Whoa, James, could you watch the swearing? I'm driving and the cell phone is on speaker; my little girl is hearing all this."*
      (Open Communication, Expressing Feelings)
  C. I became enraged. **(Friendship, Confidentiality)**
  D. I screamed "F-you." **(Mutual Respect, Fairness)**
  E. I hung up on Joe. **(Mutual Respect, Open Communication)**

Step Three: Write two Alternative Action Possibilities (AAP) that could have created a better outcome.
  A. **Core Value**: Friendship and Confidentiality
     AAP: (1) Ask if Joe is alone before speaking.
              (2) Warn Joe that this is confidential and that I want this kept between the two of us.

  B. **Core Value**: Mutual Respect
     AAP: (1) Tell Joe I would have preferred he not put me on speaker.
              (2) Ask Joe to warn me in the future if anyone else might hear our conversation.

  C. **Core Value:** Fairness
     AAP: (1) Ask myself if Joe has been unkind or doesn't have the right to ask for what he is requesting.
              (2) Ask myself if this is really important enough to lose a friend over.

  D. **Core Value**: Expressing Feelings
     AAP: (1) Compose a way I could say this with respect and consideration including my feelings, Joe's feelings, and acknowledgment of the context that he is in the car with his daughter.
              (2) I could try to work out these feelings before I say anything in anger.

  E. **Core Value**: Mutual Respect and Open Communication
     AAP: (1) I could politely say, "I'm upset and getting off the phone, but I would like to discuss this at a later time."
              (2) I could say, "I need to hang up now; let's discuss this tomorrow."

Knowing Your Core Values

In a perfect world, each individual, teacher, company, government and all the organizations in between would explicitly create a Core Value statement that they displayed and consulted when making any decision, setting any policy or planning any course of action. How many conflicts and misunderstandings could be avoided if we all wore Core Value Statement signs so the world could be forewarned of our trigger points? The main problem is that most of us are not conscious of the Core Values that trigger us most deeply.

Knowing *all* our Core Values could save us a lot of heartache. We could use them to guide us to the best people to befriend, date or marry; it could lead us to inspiring jobs and motivating careers; it could map our political, religious and philosophical journey; it could light the path for all our behavior, in all settings. Loved ones could help us stay in integrity with those values. (Our children are really good at reminding us if we don't.)

If we knew everyone's Core Values, how many landmines could we avoid in our interactions? Or, if we accidently violated someone's Core Value, we could compassionately and constructively deal with the reaction and pain of reopening those past wounds.

Below is a list of values compiled by Steve Pavlina, a motivational life coach. It might be useful to use this list to identify your Core Values and to try to rank them by priority.

Source Concepts for Core Values by Steve Pavlina

Acceptance	Fast pace	Power
Achievement	Financial rewards	Privacy
Adventure	Focus	Productivity
Altruism	Freedom	Promotion prospects
Ambition	Friendship	Reaching potential
Appreciation	Fun	Recognition
Authenticity	Happiness	Respect
Authority	Harmony	Responsibility
Autonomy	Health	Results
Balance	Helping others	Risk taking
Beauty	Honesty	Romance
Belonging	Humor	Routine

Challenge	Imagination	Security
Choice	Independence	Self-expression
Collaboration	Influence	Service
Commitment	Intellect	Sharing
Community	Intuition	Solitude
Compassion	Justice	Spirituality
Competition	Kindness	Status
Connection	Leadership	Success
Contribution	Learning	Teaching
Creativity	Love	Team work
Equality	Loyalty	Tolerance
Excellence	Making a difference	Tradition
Excitement	Nature	Travel
Expertise	Nurturing	Trust
Fairness	Order	Variety
Faith	Passion	Winning
Fame	Peace	Wisdom
Family	Personal growth	Zest for life

Excerpted from http://www.how-to-change-careers.com/personal-core-values

As will be discussed in later chapters, family behaviors, rules, traditions and values strongly influence our Core Values. We also identify our Core Values inferentially.

Emotional Reactions Can Reveal Core Values

As in the example of James and Joe, sometimes a disproportionate reaction to an event will reveal a Core Value. If we can notice and look past the event and emotions we may glimpse the Core Value (or values) that may be in play.

My reaction to the movie Slumdog Millionaire is a perfect example of how a violation of a hidden Core Value can cause serious discomfort. Intellectually, I can say that this movie is a fine production—well written, beautifully photographed, excellent performances, poignant story line. Yet, I found it so deeply disturbing, I knew it violated one or more of my Core Values. I quickly ascertained that I abhor cruelty against the innocent and powerless. I asked myself how my life reflects this Core Value. It is true that my work involves helping people, particularly the innocent and powerless. But this movie had triggered a huge reaction. Finally I understood that the movie was based on the premise that a whole society sanctioned and capitalized on cruelty against the poor and children. No amount of production value could have mitigated my emotional response to what I saw as institutionalized injustice and abuse. AND the title character's own brother perpetuated it. Here was my hidden Core Value: people with power should behave justly and compassionately. Knowing this meant that I could better understand my reactions to a range of life events since this value or its absence is often apparent in the world.

Another factor to consider when using disproportionate reactions to uncover Core Values is the history of experience with this value violation. When we have past experience with a Core Value being ignored or violated, particularly during our childhood, we are likely to have more dramatic reactions if it is violated again. In some ways, it is like the triggering flashbacks trauma survivors experience.

Jenny came to a session sobbing that she planned to break up with her fiancé, Andrew. He had arrived an hour late to pick her up the previous night. When he showed up, Jenna described telling him how upset she was over his tardiness and that there was no excuse for being so late without calling. Enraged, Andrew had yelled at her that he "...didn't deserve this, (she) was out of line to be angry, and now he didn't even want to go out with her." Jenny screamed back, "Fine, we're done then," and she slammed the door in his face.

On the surface, it seemed like Andrew had violated Jenny's Core Values around keeping a promise, or timeliness, or possibly consideration of her feelings or time. On the basis of her saying there was no excuse, she might have been referring to the value of taking responsibility for one's actions. But after questioning her, it soon became apparent that Andrew was chronically late and often failed to fulfill commitments he'd made. While Jenna didn't like these behaviors, she'd never wanted to break up over them before.

On further exploration, it turned out that Jenny had a history of not being allowed to express her feelings, particularly by men, starting with her father and brothers. When Andrew got mad at her for being upset, she re-experienced having her feelings discounted again.

Once Andrew understood that if he had just listened and acknowledged Jenny's feelings, they could have still had a pleasant evening, he was freed to notice that his response had been part of a Core Value violation of his own. He then validated her right to her feelings and apologized for being late.

Behaviors Can Reveal Core Values

Sometimes we don't notice that our behaviors reveal our Core Values. Hoping to avoid conflict, we develop strategies to reinforce the values or we ignore the negative responses those value violations elicit. Many people believe that they can fool others by pretending they are not offended, or by hiding their anger or hurt. The truth is, very little is really hidden, especially in families. Families create most of our sensitivities and wounds. Who knows better which buttons will get a reaction? Even though the real source of the discomfort may be camouflaged, the coping behavior is still noticed.

An elderly client, who'd recently lost his wife, met a prospective "date" at a bereavement group. I asked him what he liked about her. He said, "She doesn't gossip." I thought this was very interesting since it revealed a Core Value that, until then, very few of the women in his life had practiced. He revealed lifelong feelings of guilt and inauthenticity during a lifetime of enjoying his mother, sisters and wife gossip endlessly. He loved the gossipy women in his life, but listening had violated one of his Core Values. How did he cope? He had fallen asleep in the middle of conversations. He had a reputation for not listening and being forgetful. His body had developed a strategy for staying in integrity without jeopardizing his relationships.

Words Can Reveal Core Values

Neurolinguistic Programming (NLP) (Bandler, Grinder & Satir, 1976), which Satir helped create, analyzes our choice of words to understand our values, intentions and beliefs. One example of this occurs when we describe events. We unconsciously (or consciously) choose words that reveal our beliefs and values—a common criticism of news reporting, which is "supposed" to be objective.

Katherine and Andrea went to elementary school together and then did not see each other again for 40 years. Katherine had worshipped Andrea in her early years and was excited to reconnect with her childhood idol. To her bewilderment, Andrea kept referring to the fact that Katherine had skipped a grade and said that she really should have been with students a year younger. Andrea's words revealed the importance she placed on age. Her Core Value was that people belonged with others their age. By way of contrast, Katherine placed little value on age;

she had friends much older and younger than herself. Katherine valued connection and acceptance. She felt wounded that Andrea brought this issue up—it felt like it distanced Andrea from her.

Politics provides ample examples of how words and labels are used to manipulate opinions. Groups often use labels to elicit an emotional reaction to a Core Value violation, such as Pro-Choice, Right to Life, etc. When politicians call programs that help the poor "entitlement" instead of "welfare" programs, they elicit images of people who feel they are entitled to get something for nothing. Anyone with the Core Value of "Humility" or "Work Ethic," or "No Free Ride" will unavoidably be triggered by the idea of someone else being "entitled" to help without working for it.

Life Choices Can Reveal Core Values

Sometimes, we reveal our Core Values through our life choices, or the rules we follow. For instance, every religion seems to espouse some version of the Golden Rule that says "treat others as you would treat yourself." Many people live by this rule without understanding that the Core Value of the rule is about feeling and acting with compassion and empathy, because that is how they want to be treated. Some of us are much nicer to others than we are to ourselves. Perhaps this injunction is meant for the people who save the best for themselves and give others inferior quality or service. Rules should be evaluated for context and appropriateness, as well as the insights they provide into the real Core Value underlying it.

Once we identify Core Values, our reactions change and our future choices are more likely to reflect our deepest beliefs and needs. We can choose to set boundaries that proactively protect us from Core Value violations. "Please ask before you borrow something that is mine" (Core Value: taking care of possessions and respectfulness) or "Please clean up after yourself before I get home" (Core Value: thoughtfulness, cleanliness or both). We may not always get our requests honored, but we can know when our anger and hurt is current or from an ancient experience.

The good news is that once something is brought into our consciousness, it loses its need to stay hidden. Knowing our Core Values guides us to make appropriate choices for better outcomes in the future as opposed to repeating history again and again.

For example: "Since I hate to wait for people and you don't seem to mind, call me when you get there and I'll come right away" (Core Value: Not wasting time, timeliness, or respect for others' time.)

Acting in Integrity with Your Core Values

In the context of this book, the word "*integrity*" means "our words, thoughts and behaviors are consistent with our Core Values." When they aren't consistent, when our words, thoughts or actions don't reflect our Core Values, we can't feel good about ourselves.

INTEGRITY:

Core Values match…

What we THINK (beliefs, ideas, meanings)

What we SAY (rules, philosophies, teachings)

What we DO (behaviors, affiliations)

It is easier to see when someone is **not** acting in integrity with their Core Values than when they are. While they might feel guilty or depressed, they also might be rationalizing their behavior or in denial. When any word or behavior suggests hypocrisy, it is a clear signal that we are not in integrity with our Core Values.

> *An event occurred at the Satir Family Camp that illustrates the conflicts that can occur even in a community dedicated to preserving the Core Values of its members. One year the camp was asked to participate in filming a documentary about Virginia Satir. A discussion ensued to decide whether the director, one of the late therapist's closest friends and also a former camper, could come into camp to film.*
>
> *The camp had a policy of limiting camp access to current campers (Core Value: keeping everyone safe—both emotionally and physically.) They also had a tradition of making decisions by consensus (Core Value: open communication and considering the needs of each individual.) In keeping with these Core Values, the facilitator, who personally valued unanimous support, stated that all campers must agree to the filming or it wouldn't be allowed.*
>
> *Hours of community discussion followed. Most of the camp members were very enthusiastic about the filming because it fit their personal Core Values of inclusiveness, providing a forum, or perpetuating Satir's vision. Some campers didn't have an opinion and didn't participate in the lengthy sessions. Other campers were happy to support the majority because they valued pleasing people, keeping peace and compromising. A few were willing to tolerate the filming*

> *under certain circumstances that protected their privacy. That left one unmoving dissenter, Lilith, who maintained that her Core Value, "the sacredness of camp," would be violated by allowing the filming.*
>
> *In keeping with the facilitator's stated intention to gain unanimous support, Lilith's stance stopped the filming. There was significant dissatisfaction with this decision, partly because the facilitator had unilaterally proposed this rule, but also because many of the proponents questioned the motives of the dissenter. They did not share her reasoning that the filming (especially under strictly supervised, limited conditions) would do anything to hurt the "sacredness of camp."*
>
> *Ironically, on the final evening of camp, Lilith and her husband were found violating one of camp's few nonnegotiable rules. Many people were outraged by this violation—not because the rule had been broken, but because Lilith had opposed the filming, and then, by breaking the camp rule, had violated her stated Core Value of maintaining the sacredness of camp by breaking the camp's Core Value of following camp rules.*

Applying Core Value Awareness to Relationships

When two Core Values are violated at the same time, most relationships will experience a crisis. Couples in love often don't discuss the unconscious factors that craft our dreams and life goals. Yet knowing family history, expectations, roles, rules and Core Values are essential to ensuring a smooth ride into the couple's future together. That is not to say that these goals and dreams don't change over the years. But most of the time (barring traumatic or otherwise life-changing events), Core Values tend to stay consistent over time. Changes mainly occur in how they are manifested as behaviors or goals. So it is wise to understand a potential partner's Core Values before making any commitments, so that potential conflicts can be anticipated and addressed.

> *John's Core Value is independence. He likes to decide what he is going to do and when he is going to do it. Wendy's Core Value is being considered and considerate. She usually considers the opinions and needs of others, and wants her needs to be considered. Most of the time, John and Wendy discussed plans and their Core Values were compatible. Since Wendy is considerate of John's choices, he will most likely get what he wants, and, as long as there is discussion, she will feel considered. Problems occur when John makes a unilateral decision without discussing it with Wendy. When Wendy gets triggered into objecting, John becomes triggered into making the meaning that Wendy's needs threaten his independence. Proactive planning avoids the conflict.*

Many of the most effective models in Couples Therapy, such as Harville Hendrix' Imago Therapy (1988), address Core Value violations as the source (and solution) to marital conflict. Because most people have many Core Values, the solution to a problem can sometimes be found in identifying the particular value that can produce a compatible outcome.

> *Jason and Sandy went through a crisis that lasted several years because of a strong Core Value conflict. Jason held the Core Value that it was important to share deep emotional connections with as many people as possible, both men and women. As an introvert, this meant Jason wanted to have emotional relationships with people other than his wife. Sandy's Core Value was that a man and wife should fulfill all of each other's needs exclusively. In practice that meant a man and woman should only express love and emotional intimacy with each other. They both agreed on a physically monogamous relationship, but they disagreed about emotional connections with others. Eventually, Jason realized that he and Sandy shared another Core Value: Honoring Commitment. He was able to sacrifice his desire for close emotional relations with others in service of their shared value of Honoring Commitment. Additionally, he values keeping Sandy happy and avoiding the consequences of her unhappiness. At this point in their relationship, Jason has decided that Honoring Commitment is a more important Core Value than experiencing deep emotional connections with others outside his marriage.*

Ultimately, we must understand and keep integrity with our Core Values to ensure our work, home, friendships and families authentically represent who we are. Many of us can live out of integrity for long periods of time, especially when one Core Value supersedes another, such as in Jason and Sandy's example.

The internet is replete with websites related to Core Values; they are generally managed by business coaches emphasizing how our professional life must be consonant with our Core Values. The focus on the work domain is not surprising since it is the most common place that people forsake their Core Values for other rewards. Perhaps this is one reason so many people complain that they are not happy in their careers. Knowledge is power. First you have to identify *what* you value and then you can decide *how* you will live in integrity with it.

Worksheet for Chapter 9: Core Values - Defining what is important to you

Question: What are your Core Values?

Activity: Create a timeline of positive and important life events. Identify the Core Value you learned or employed in three of the most significant experiences listed.

Example:

Age:	1 yr.	5yr.	19yr.
Event:	#1) walked without help	#2) Sister Born	#3) changed College major

Core Value: #1) Working hard and practice can get you independence

#2) There is enough love for everyone

#3) It's important to follow your heart

Age:

Event:

Core Values:

  #1

  #2

  #3

Practice: When you make a decision, or get upset, notice the Core Value that is embedded in your reaction or choice.

Challenge: Evaluate whether your life choices are in integrity with your Core Values

Chapter Ten: Assessment

"The greatest gift I can give is to see, hear, understand, and touch another person."
– Virginia Satir

From the moment children are born, we are assessing them based on a whole range of physical and developmental milestones, starting with their APGAR scores (a number that tells medical staff how healthy a child is at birth) and continuing throughout childhood with various achievement and intelligence tests. Our children are evaluated again and again on scales meant to compare them with other children their chronological age. Knowledge of their accomplishments and when they have achieved them is used to decide what they should learn and when it should be taught.

Unfortunately, most children don't display "normal" consistent, linear development. Very intelligent children often have highly asynchronous development. Highly and Profoundly Gifted children can have the cognitive skills of a college student, the motor skills of a young child, and the emotional skills of something in between. Children may have learning disabilities that limit their potential to achieve or even demonstrate what they already know. Even average children have challenges and gifts that often get overlooked during traditional evaluations.

Unfortunately numbers such as test scores only tell a part of the story. When social, emotional, educational or language challenges impede achievement, standardized test scores reveal only a small part of the child's potential. Test administrators can't always compensate for these obstacles, and some don't even consider them when reporting test results. Other factors, such as attention, personality, learning style, behavior, health, emotions and lack of rapport with the tester, can also undermine the outcome of any quantitative tests. Most importantly, our children are more than what they can demonstrate; they are unique individuals with potential qualities, needs, and gifts that define them.

Satir placed a lot of weight upon nurturing high self-esteem. She referred to having good feelings about ourselves as having a "full pot" and a poor sense of self as having an "empty pot." As discussed in previous chapters, an important factor in having a strong positive sense of self includes feeling seen, heard and accepted for who you are as opposed to what you have done or failed to do. Frequently, test results are used to limit our opportunities to learn who we are and what we are capable of doing. Over time, this can drain that self-esteem "pot."

The more environments challenge, nurture, and celebrate a child's gifts, the more likely they will thrive. We all want to be appreciated for our gifts, even if they are hidden; to feel lovable for all that makes us unique even if we don't perform well in certain areas or under certain circumstances, is a universal yearning. Qualitative assessments are one way to identify a child's qualities and to understand their potential.

Qualitative Approaches to Assessment

Any method of evaluation that does not quantify or measure something can be considered qualitative. As the root of the term implies, it is an evaluation of quality (or qualities), usually taking into account context and implications. Qualitative methods of assessment have been used to assess products, programs, performance, proposals, research, organizations, and people, for a variety of purposes.

Qualitative assessments of children usually use in-depth, unstructured interviews, history, observation and interaction directly with the child to fill in the picture of his or her needs. These assessments are performed by professional counselors, therapists, psychologists, or learning specialists with a background in teaching and educational environments.

The particular approach used depends upon the purpose of the evaluation and also the particular orientation of the assessor. For example, a teacher or school administrator may primarily look for information related to the child's ability to learn, fit in with other children in the classroom, follow teacher instructions and function at school; someone trained in identifying learning disabilities may be especially alert for overt or hidden problems that could stem from auditory, visual, and sensory modality weaknesses, as well as challenges with attention, concentration, impulse control, social skills, eye-hand coordination, language and communication; a behavior specialist may be watching for potential ways to reinforce socially acceptable behaviors and extinguish socially unacceptable behaviors. The usefulness of these qualitative assessment techniques depends upon the skill, judgment, experience, orientation and insights of the individual professional performing the evaluation, not to mention the nature of the findings and recommendations that accompany these observations.

Whole Child Assessment (WCA) — A Qualitative Assessment

Qualitative testing is not generally used as a substitute for quantitative tests because intelligence and achievement are also part of the richness the child brings to the world. It complements standardized testing by collecting information about traits that are more difficult to quantify, such as emotional, spiritual, and temperamental processes, personality, and learning style. All of these factors help us appreciate and reinforce a child's unique approach to life. By synthesizing a spectrum of information from family history, developmental milestones, background information, inventories completed by the parents (e.g., personality, overexcitabilities, learning challenge screeners, characteristics of giftedness), interviews, play therapy, in-depth observation, and other types of unstructured but strategic interactions, it is easier to fully understand the child's needs, challenges and gifts—that which Satir described as "the person who is called by your name."

Recommendations derived from qualitative analyses allow parents to gain better awareness of which environments and parenting styles would have a high probability of helping their child achieve a happy and fulfilling life experience. All this information is important and relevant to fully understanding and fulfilling the needs of a particular child.

Gifts to Notice, Appreciate and Optimize

Emotional	Ethical	Intellectual
Spiritual	Personal	Insights
Creative	Personality	Physical
Maturity	Judgment	Perception

Whole Child Assessment is an example of a qualitative assessment that is a synthesis of the models, techniques and philosophies of many experts in the world of assessment, psychology, education and philosophy—including Virginia Satir, Carl Jung, Jean Piaget, Kazimierz Dabrowski, Martin Buber, Maria Montessori, Annemarie Roeper, and particularly Linda Silverman. Developed because families often needed more information than quantitative assessments could provide, it is another way to understand and acknowledge a child's gifts. Parents wanting concrete recommendations on how to optimize these gifts—how best to love, educate and appreciate these emerging human beings—find qualitative approaches more user-friendly, both to them, and to their child. WCA is one way to fulfill Satir's goal of seeing, hearing and understanding our children.

At just 4½ Maya had a reputation. She had already been asked to leave three nursery schools (her first day there) and two playgroups. She had offended all the neighbors, yet was adored by several adults who were charmed by her original ideas, and precocious eloquence. Her parents loved her deeply, but were worn out by her emotional reactivity and seemingly random "melt downs." "Be prepared," they warned, "she doesn't like very many people."

Before interviewing her, I had asked Maya's parents to tell her a lady who helps kids was coming over to play with her, that she would be in charge of what we would do, and that I wanted to get to know her. Her parents greeted me with hugs (having already bonded during the times we'd met to discuss their concerns and observations). Maya hid behind the drapes. I noticed an elaborate Lego construction (obviously a Maya creation) and started asking questions about it. Maya groaned dramatically as she drew aside the drapes, "I am the ONLY one who can answer those questions," she sighed, and began to enthusiastically answer questions. When she paused, I dropped to her eye level, introduced myself, and offered to shake hands. She stared at my hand a second, and then skipped off in the direction of her room, yelling over her shoulder, "Come look at THIS." I followed her and she talked non-stop for an hour and fifteen minutes. During that time, Maya introduced me to her world: explaining challenges, asking questions of me (many of them very personal), responding to my queries, climbing into my lap, touching my hair and face, and explaining her theories about why some people don't like her. She bid me farewell with a big hug.

During the feedback session with her parents, I explained that Maya is a fascinating mix of asynchronous development, cognitive complexity, boundary challenges, and emotions that travel all over the map. In Maya's case, she was dealing with both challenges (Twice Exceptional), as well as the rare condition of Prosopagnosia (face blindness) which impairs the ability to remember and read facial features for meaning. Once her parents understood both her gifts (she was more cognitively advanced and creative than they'd understood) and her challenges (Prosopagnosia and autism can both cause high anxiety, paranoid vigilance and emotional reactivity) they found the empathy and compassion that had been eluding them in dealing with her quixotic reactions. They decided to homeschool Maya so that they could provide positive (but highly consistent and controlled) social interactions while feeding her voracious intellectual appetite at her own advanced pace.

As parents, most of us yearn for a "guide" to our particular child, to know what is "normal," what is special, and when to panic. Assessments such as WCA provide a range of information that is useful in many settings, but particularly in making educational decisions. Because of this any test report should be written to provide direction to schools or treatment teams, as well as to guide parents through an immediate action plan, if necessary. Most important, the assessment process can help parents view their children through a new, relatively objective set of eyes—ones with an overview of how other similar children have achieved their optimum life experience and fulfilled their potential.

Whole Child Assessment – The General Process

1) Initial Interview
   - Initial contact with parents (by email, phone, or in-person)
   - Parents complete forms, histories, scales, anecdotal history, and inventories.

2) Session One: Parents (by email, phone, or in-person)
   - Review and discussion of all information submitted
   - Clarification of questions
   - Exploration of hopes and expectations

3) Session Two: The Child (in-person only)
   - Welcome and introduction
   - Honoring the child with choices for interaction that include:
     - Who?
       - Alone with me
       - With family members (siblings or one or both parents) included
     - What?
       - Play (what type – imaginative, games, or activities – and who initiates it)
       - Demonstration (of interests, achievements, skills)
       - Discussion (interactive, expository, projective, cognitive, emotional)
       - Art activity (joint, individual, expressive or interpretive) or physical activity (competitive, cooperative or demonstrative)
     - When?
       - Timeframe for each interaction
     - Where?
       - In child's home (bedroom, outside, playroom)
       - In my home office or other office
     - How?
       - Interactive
       - Passive
       - Initiating
   - Observing the child's environment
     - Home: bedroom, play areas, work areas, etc.
     - School (if parents contract for classroom observation)
   - Engaging the child in the activities chosen
   - Discussing child's interests and concerns while interacting

4) Session Three: Feedback to Parents (by email, phone, or in-person)
   - Discussion of findings
   - Questions and clarifications
   - Creating an action plan for going forward

5) Written Report (optional)
   - Approximately 6 weeks later
   - Meeting to discuss details, answer questions
   - Amendments depending upon intended use

There are many variations as to the type of report a parent might need. Some parents are happy with an oral explanation of what was observed and their implications. Others want a detailed written explanation of what happened and what conclusions were reached and why. Some parents plan to share the report with the school, or with other families. In all cases, it is useful to understand the child and his or her own unique gifts and challenges.

The Whole Child Assessment Report

- Introduction to process
- Background of child
- Family history
- Reasons for assessment
- Initial impressions
- Summary of observations
- Lists of skills and strengths
- Findings on:
  - Temperament and Sensitivities
  - Learning Style
  - Personality Typology
  - Behavioral Style
  - IQ range estimate
- Lists and explanation of challenges
- Discussion of results
- Summary
- Recommendations

Potential Benefits of Qualitative Assessment

- Gain new appreciation for the child's gifts
- Receive validation or clarification of observations
- Understand ramifications of child's gifts and challenges
- Absorb insights into child's motivations and behaviors
- Identify systemic patterns and puzzles
- Gain strategies to address frustrations and avoid landmines
- Learn new ways to optimize gifts and strengths
- Increase potential for addressing hidden challenges
- Modeling of parenting and family governance techniques

Candice said that she knew her parents really loved her because they acknowledged what they valued in her every day. Each morning her mother greeted her with a broad smile and the statement, "I'm so happy to see you, I've been waiting for you to wake up all morning. I just love the way you……." and she would say something nice so Candice started her day happy. At night, her father ended her days by telling her, "Today the gift you gave me was the gift of…………" and each night he filled in the blank with something related to what Candice had done or said: the gift of laughter, the gift of insight, the gift of sunshine. She would go to sleep thinking about all the ways she might have given him that gift, and what she could give him the next day.

Worksheet for Chapter Ten: Assessment

Question: *What qualities define you and the members of your family?*

Activity: *For each member of your family write four positive words to describe who they are (as opposed to what they do or have achieved), and what you mean by the description.*

<u>Name / Relationship</u>   <u>Description</u>
e.g. Michael /   *funny- can find the humor in a situation*
    son   *creative- has original ideas, has made up stories forever*
   emotional- cares about people, things, opinions
   passionate- believes in something with all his heart
   ethical- dislikes hypocrisy, is sensitive to phoniness

A. 1.
    2.
    3.
    4.

B. 1.
    2.
    3.
    4.

C. 1.
    2.
    3.
    4.

D. 1.
    2.
    3.
    4.

Challenge: *Have all family members make a similar list; compare and contrast perceptions among different family members.*

Part Four: Old Business, New Possibilities

"We can learn something new anytime we believe we can." —*Virginia Satir*

Chapter Eleven: Past, Present, and Future

"Learn to exchange judging for exploring, being right for being real, anxiety for excitement, and limitations for possibilities."
— Virginia Satir

Traditionally psychotherapy focused on past events, based on the often correct assumption that they were the real source of reactions to current challenges. The theory was that once people understood the source of their problems, insight alone would alleviate any current symptoms. While Satir understood the value of making unconscious motivations and beliefs conscious, she also understood that there is a complex relationship between knowledge and change. Many factors affect how influential past experiences turn out to be. Such variables as personality, beliefs, family rules, resilience, coping mechanisms, attitudes, extremity of the event, meanings elicited by the experience, and external resources are all ingredients in a recipe that feeds our reactions. As discussed in previous chapters, we often experience current challenges with reactions that are really responses to old memories flavored with unresolved feelings (both conscious and unconscious).

> *Beth had a history of failed relationships. As soon as it seemed the relationship was getting serious, she'd start an argument over something minor, and then use it as an excuse to break up. While examining her family history, she related how her childhood had been spent with her father coming in and out of her life. As soon as she would start to get to know him, he would disappear for a few years. From this experience she'd developed the expectation that if she cared about a man, he would leave soon. To avoid the pain she had experienced repeatedly as a child, she unconsciously developed a coping mechanism that protected her from being abandoned. This awareness was the first step towards changing that pattern so that she could potentially enter a relationship of love and trust.*

Children Need Positive Attachment to Feel Okay in the World

Most of us start life caring what our caregivers think about us. Even at a few months, we reward attention with smiles and giggles in the hope that we will receive mirrored reactions. These early smiles communicate appreciation and are the forerunners of the connection we seek the rest of our lives. But sometimes that interaction doesn't happen, or happens in a damaged way. Primary caregivers can fail to nurture healthy attachment for many reasons—they may be too busy, punitive, neglectful, tired, sick, anxious, self-absorbed, selfish or resentful of the baby's needs; they may have unrealistic expectations of what the child would mean to them, or how it would behave—projecting a message of disappointment when the child cannot fulfill these unreasonable expectations.

Sometimes there is a problem with a child's ability to connect—autism or sensory sensitivity can make the child unresponsive or hyper-reactive, not allowing healthy attachment to occur. Equally disruptive but especially poignant, are situations when the parent is unable to connect because of social, emotional or physical challenges such as depression, schizophrenia, autism, chronic illness, developmental disabilities, or substance abuse. These are just a few of the conditions that can prevent a healthy attached relationship from growing between a child and his or her primary caregivers. Each of these can affect the quality of connection in all future relationships.

People have children for all kinds of reasons and their behavior as parents may or may not reflect those reasons. When teenage girls say they want a baby so they will have someone to love them unconditionally, I recommend they get a dog instead. None of us can know, in advance, all that motherhood entails—both the good and the challenging. And teenagers are not even developmentally prepared for the wear and tear of parenting.

Ultimately, we all use a combination of positive and less than positive ways to deal with parenting challenges. Many of us know our own experiences were lacking and seek help to learn better strategies. Some of us are sent by agencies, friends or relatives to learn better ways to help our children thrive. Some see children suffering and have no clue what can be done to improve. But whatever inspires us to get help doesn't change the process; we need to understand the history and set a new course toward achieving a better future. The hardest part is staying present and acting in the "now" so that this process has a chance to be fulfilled.

> *Cindy, a single mom, came to therapy to help her very depressed pre-teen daughter, Rachel. In the course of explaining Rachel's depression, Cindy saw herself and the parallels in her own childhood and subsequent poor relationship with her own mother. Her mother had been emotionally unavailable, self-absorbed, and distant. Cindy said she had run out of ideas and both relationships were awful, but she began to see that her relationship with herself also needed some healing. As she began to try new behaviors she remembered past events, beliefs and fears that kept her locked in old habits. Having someone care about her, her daughter, her life, healed her heart enough to hear and practice new possibilities.*
>
> *Soon both Cindy and Rachel reported how much happier they were. They burst out laughing when asked how they had accomplished this: "Oh," Cindy giggled, "whenever we have a problem, Rachel and I brainstorm together. As soon as we imagine 'What would Linda do?' our mood lifts and together we construct a more*

positive strategy." This could only happen when Cindy felt loved enough to relate to Rachel with an open heart.

Creating Positive Connection with Children

I believe that if parents are fair, loving, respectful and consistent in dealing with their children, the result will be positive connection and trust. Of course, consistency is not always easy, because it isn't just about keeping promises and following through on threats. Consistency is a manifestation of staying in integrity. Described earlier with congruent behavior, living with integrity means that what you say, think and do match. As a parent, it means modeling behaviors that reflect the values you expect your children to practice (such as not lying or hitting anyone if you expect them to be truthful and not hit peers or siblings.)

Denise complained bitterly about how disrespectful her 7 year-old son is to her. "He doesn't pay attention when I ask him to do something, and he doesn't do it, even if I ask several times." The whole time she was describing these behaviors, her son was begging her to take him to the restroom—she intermittently ignored his pleas, and glared at him. She didn't address him at all until he took off, at which time, she screamed at him for running away.

Our children watch everything we do. Growing up and maturing depends on identifying patterns and rules. Our children are consciously or unconsciously comparing what we teach to what we practice at all stages of life. Any disparity results in loss of trust. Once trust is lost, it is a steep climb to reclaim it. The kind of consistency that includes integrity between values, words and deeds is most likely to result in the kind of human beings we hope our children to be.

Deciding How to Be

Most of us develop our ideas about how to be in the world at a very young age. We observe the adults and siblings around us and make decisions based on limited experience and immature judgment. We adopt survival strategies based on early experiences at a time when we are completely dependent upon others for our survival. One baby learns that if he cries loudly enough, relief will appear. This can translate into a belief that only "the squeaky wheel gets the grease." Another learns that his cries will go unheeded and becomes a pessimist, assuming his needs will never be met. When these early messages are transferred into later behaviors, change can only occur with insight into their source followed by creation of a new belief and behavioral response.

Because the world of a child is limited and self-centered, perceptions are necessarily self-absorbed and self-preserving. This is developmentally appropriate. Human beings are slow to become self-sufficient so they must have survival skills and tenacity to survive childhood. These early learned survival messages are difficult to transform, especially if new, more effective behaviors and habits have never been reinforced.

Ideally developmental growth occurs in us when we expand our focus, explore new environments and learn new ways of coping and being. Unfortunately, some of us never progress to later developmental stages or achieve a more mature focus and coping strategies. When this happens we remain stuck in strategies that are obsolete, or don't fit our new challenges. This is usually caused when early attachments proved insecure, and developmental needs were not fulfilled.

> *Annie was raised by a single mom who was a drug addict. By the time she was moved into foster care, she had learned that to get attention and care, she had to be cooperative, charming and affectionate. Even then, the rewards were intermittent, but still served to keep this behavior strongly embedded as her "winning formula" for getting what she needed. This strategy worked pretty well until she began to date. This saying "yes" to any request, regardless of what she wanted resulted in a pregnancy scare. Teen boys did not understand the sources of her affection and charm. They were happy to ask her to do what they wanted, and suddenly cooperation had negative repercussions. With support, she could understand the source of her strategy and design a more value and context-appropriate approach.*

It's Not What Happens to Us — It's How We React to What Happens

Many of us have lived through horrific childhoods, sometimes because of physical or emotional abuse or neglect, sometimes because of circumstances. Even in abuse cases, different people may have completely different reactions. The National Research Council estimates child sexual abuse rates range from a low of 20-24 percent to a high of 54-62 percent of the population[1]. Many of us carry the scars of abuse, but just as many have moved beyond it, refusing to feel like a victim and creating a powerful response and even helping others get past their experiences. There are many ways to heal from past negative experiences. Most of us decide to do just that, even if we need help to do so.

---

[1] National Research Council, *Understanding Child Abuse and Neglect,* page 94, Washington, DC: National Academy Press, 1993.
http://www.nap.edu/openbook.php?record_id=2117&page=94 (March 20, 2013)

Satir stressed that the problem is not what happens to us, but what we do and feel about what has happened. This is quite an empowering belief. It implies we are in charge of our feelings and responses. Her models reinforced that idea by helping people identify the ways we control our reactions by making meanings of our experiences. Our attitudes, feelings and how we interpret what happens to us can be as important to shaping our response as the event itself. The obvious example of this is how different people, even in the same family, react to the same event.

> *A successful young woman described her brother as a loser, unable to keep a job or maintain a relationship. When asked what her parents were like, she described them as critical and distant; nothing she or her brother did was ever good enough to please them. When asked why she thought she had escaped her brother's fate, she replied that at a very early age, she saw her parents criticize her perfectly reasonable brother. At that moment she decided that if they were wrong about him, they must be wrong about everything; so she ignored everything they said to criticize her. In fact, she was motivated to prove them wrong. Her brother believed the criticism, and fulfilled their dire predictions.*

The ability to bounce back from disappointment or failure is called resilience. An individual's resilience is affected by many factors besides early experiences; these can include intelligence, physical and emotional well-being, availability of support systems, beliefs, and our perceptions; each of which significantly impact resilience. Even innate personality traits, such as anxiety or perfectionism, can make one person more resilient than the next. No matter what the reason, we can still strengthen our resilience by changing how we perceive or interpret an event. The exercise for this chapter demonstrates how a new way of looking at an old understanding can change our feelings.

Worksheet for Chapter 11: Past, Present and Future

Activity: List two decisions in your life that were influenced by past experiences, next follow it up with a new awareness and future behavior possibility.

Example:

Past Influence:

I selected a wife who was controlling, like my mother…

Present Awareness

I can choose to appreciate why I might want that in my life…

Future Possibility:

I appreciate my wife, who is capable of being in control and competent…

Practice Exercise #1:

Past Influence:

Present Awareness:

Future Possibility:

Practice Exercise #2:

Past Influence:

Present Awareness

Future Possibility

Chapter Twelve: Parents and Others

"What children get is what their parents have to offer... It is often only incomplete, distorted or denied as far as the fulfillment of life is concerned. What is so hopeful about this is that which is incomplete can be completed, distorted can be straightened, and that which is denied can be revealed; unless a human being has literally had his brain cut out, all these changes are possible."
— *Virginia Satir*

Therapeutic transformation of relationships starts with understanding emotional responses between people: parents and their children; ourselves and other family members, co-workers or friends. Sometimes all of the people in the relationship are physically present, but usually they are not. It is useful when all the players can be present to explain what they mean; their real intentions (as opposed to what we imagined their motivation to be); to clarify what they remember from the past; to provide information that was missing; and, especially, when they can promise to try to change. When there is someone to facilitate these painful discussions—to keep everyone focused, listening, and being mutually respectful and kind—great progress can be made in healing and moving past ancient wounds.

Family Therapy – A New Systemic Approach

Satir pioneered the practice of Family Therapy in which whole families worked together to resolve differences and improve relationships. Before Satir, each member might have had his or her own therapist, or one family member might have been considered "the problem" or the "identified patient" (IP), but the only discussions between family members—if they occurred at all—occurred later at home, without facilitation. This type of therapy focused on one person's problem. Satir saw the problem as a symptom of poor communication and coping in the family system. She looked for solutions that could be reinforced with the support and help of the people who lived with the person. This worked because solutions depend upon changing behavior and perception—the client doesn't live in a vacuum. Satir named this family therapy process Conjoint Family Therapy. It is a type of Systems Therapy, based on Systems Theory. According to Systems Therapy, the system is perpetuating the dysfunction in the individual. Solutions come from individuals in the context of the dysfunctional system, and success depends upon how the individual interacts with the system.

In Conjoint Family Therapy, the entire family is present in the therapy room and works with the therapist to gain new insights, develop more realistic or productive ways of communicating when there are conflicts, and most importantly, how to listen to each other's feelings in more productive ways. Conjoint Family Therapy can help parents and children use more positive strategies to relate with each other.

Families come to Conjoint Therapy with beliefs and presumptions about how things are "supposed to be" and about each other. The identified patient (IP) is thought to be "*the problem that needs to be fixed.*" All family members fear that they will get blamed or criticized, and the IP fears everyone already believes he or she is the one who needs to change. In Conjoint Family Therapy, a basic principle is that the current system perpetuates the problem; the IP just acts it out. Using this approach, the system is analyzed, changes proposed and practiced, and eventually family members find a new process for relating that relieves the stress that has destabilized the whole.

"The Problem" that the family has internalized generally turns out to be a story that has been told and retold until it seems like the only truth. Once "the story" becomes just one option, it frees characters to feel and express their loving feelings (under the hurt ones). Everyone works together to write new chapters and a new ending. When the extreme language of the story—"always, never, can't, won't"—turns into kinder, empathetic expressions of understanding and underlying sadness and hurt, the new story begins. The anger, frustration and hurt elicited by the old story melt in the hope that these new possibilities will work. Even families that have tremendous challenges—mental illness, learning disorders, physical disabilities, economic challenges—find that the whole family can be more powerful than each of its parts. If they can work together towards finding solutions, if they know that they share the same goals of getting along and loving each other, they are able to make the transformation towards healthier relationships. This transformation is more likely to occur under the guidance of a facilitator, because an outsider has the benefit of seeing the big picture, without the insider's habits and belief history.

Steps of a Conjoint Family Therapy Meeting
(When an Event is the Source of Conflict)

Step One: Select an experienced Family Therapist
Select a therapist with experience in Conjoint Family Therapy who can keep the room safe for all family members, and who has an orientation towards creating a solution for the future (as opposed to letting the family stay focused on the problems and behaviors of the past).

Step Two: Enlist family in plan to meet for a session
Get all members of the family system to agree to come together to discuss the problem with a family therapist. It is best if all participants feel that the therapist is neutral and won't take sides. Participants can ask the therapist questions in advance to address fears and concerns.

Step Three: Meet with therapist to learn necessary new skills
At the session, the therapist may create a Genogram or Family Map (See Chapter 2) to place members in relation to each other. Sometimes seating in the room can be reorganized to help support younger or weaker members (e.g., when a child is the IP, the therapist may choose to sit on one side of the child, and place the most supportive parent on the other, so the child can feel protected and supported in having a voice).

The therapist will create a supportive environment and alert the participants about specific elements to be listening for:
1) Relevant information some of the participants might not know (such as something that happened before they arrived, or even before they were born).
2) Incongruities (e.g., things that are being said that might not convey what the person really means or wanted to say, or was actually thinking and feeling).
3) Unmet needs. The story is never really the problem. Participants need to be alert for the underlying unmet needs a person really is responding to, so that they can help the person find a better way to ask for that in the future.

Step Four: Appreciations and observations
The therapist may ask members to each state one wish for the session, and write it down on the Genogram, or may ask each person to provide one trait he or she likes about other family members. In this process, the Genogram starts to grow into a resource and picture of the parts as well as the whole family. *Note: Appreciations open the heart so people can hear with love instead of fear.*

Step Five: The therapist models setting boundaries to create a safe space for the work
The therapist states the rules of communication for the session, such as:

1) No "put downs" or name calling. Banned words include "always, never, refuses ..." Family members can add potential problem words.
2) One person speaks at a time, after the therapist recognizes the speaker *(sometimes raising hands or passing a talking stick helps).*
3) The goal is to express feelings with compassion and kindness, as opposed to blaming.

Step Six: The therapist guides the family in new ways of expressing and listening to feelings. Examples of roles:
1) Scribe (a volunteer, or someone not directly involved in the story) – writes or draws the story step-by-step, noting what people say about the "scenes."
2) Story Teller (group can decide who) – tells what happened frame by frame; interviews participants to determine how they felt at the time, and what this reminded them of from their past.

3) Observers (therapist is one, and family members can volunteer) – take notes on patterns, process, misunderstandings, and potential changes for future interactions.

Step Seven: The family discusses their story, gently guided by the therapist.
Family members agree on the story to be discussed. Under the direction of the therapist, they jointly begin to paint a picture of the event or situation. Using the recommended tools and strategies, the family adds details and looks for clues about patterns, needs, misunderstandings, values and feelings. The therapist helps to keep the family focused and guarantee the safety of the environment by making sure that each member is respected and heard. While the therapist may provide the brush and canvas, the family paints the painting.

Step Eight: Neutral feedback to make the unconscious past habits conscious
1) Observers report what they noticed about each part of the story, identify themes, and patterns (similar to how an anthropologist observes).
2) Group is surveyed for more information about those themes, patterns or observations.
3) Participants have the opportunity to ask questions that anyone still has about feelings, intentions, and motivations.
4) Participants answer these questions.
5) Questioners repeat what they heard to check that they understood the answer.
6) The therapist ascertains from all participants any new information that might have been learned and what difference it might have made in their feelings about the event or the person.

Step Nine: Feedback, insights and hopes

Participants all express something new they learned or noticed. They are invited to express a hope or wish for a change about the future.

When the parents are not physically present, healing old wounds can still occur. What is really healing about working on old wounds is being able to talk about them without being shamed. That allows us the opportunity of entertaining a possibility that our painful beliefs about them were wrong, or that, at least, our parents loved us and didn't hurt us on purpose.

Parents Do the Best They Can

Satir maintained that parents are the best parents they know how to be. That is not to say that many parents don't make terrible mistakes in raising their children. Sometimes they fall prey to bad advice, mental illness, ignorance, narcissism, weakness or recreating their own early experiences. Luckily, most of us recover from childhood wounds and go on to experience and create positive, caring relationships. We find ways to move on, develop more positive ways of parenting, and we try not to make the same mistakes. The journey toward wholeness and improvement—not repeating unhealthy patterns for the next generation—takes a conscious awareness that there is another choice. Unfortunately, most families are dealing with unconscious emotional wounds and sometimes family secrets. Often the relief comes from gaining a new understanding of the parent, the family secret, and a reframing of the lessons we learn from our own early experiences.

> *Mary did not like gifts. She didn't like to buy them or receive them, and she really didn't like to open them in front of anyone. She explained that she was raised by her single father, a bachelor father, and she had four older brothers. There were no traditions, no holidays, no decorations and very few gifts, even for birthdays. She never learned how to buy a present, and her brothers teased her when she opened any that she received. This left her very self-conscious, believing that she must not have been good enough for Santa to bring anything or for anyone to remember her birthday with a party like the other girls would have. When we studied her father's genogram and examined his family of origin, it became apparent that he'd probably had a similar experience and thought it completely normal. He was the last of 13 boys; the only daughter of the family was born soon after him. Not only was his mother probably quite worn out by then, but the novelty of a daughter must have left very little attention for that last son. He had raised his family to match his own experience. Once Mary understood her father's likely experience, she could forgive her father for not knowing any better, and she'd made sure that her children had birthdays and parties, and holidays while they were growing up. The multi-generational pattern ended with Mary's effort. Now, armed with her new belief that she deserved gifts as much as anyone does, Mary could consciously start a new tradition of buying herself something she wanted every birthday and Christmas.*

Healing Old Wounds

Healing old wounds in families involves creating new family rules that empower all members to ask for their needs to be met, as well as the mechanism to understand and accommodate diverse core values and needs. It is important to heal wounds within oneself, even if one's family cannot be healed. The wounds occur in the context of the family system, but the healing must take place within the individual.

> *Lynne was adopted at birth by two older, very quiet and conservative parents. They loved her but were confounded by her desire to take risks, to be unconventional and rebellious. Lynne always felt bad about her need to be boisterous, wild,*

> and "edgy," as she called it; she was stuck in a story of not fitting in because her parents disapproved of her personality.
>
> After her parents died, she used the internet to find her birth father. Welcomed with open arms, she traveled to meet him and his children. She was amazed at how comfortable she felt with them. She fit perfectly into this enthusiastic, tattooed, wild, fun-loving family. Finally understanding that her personality was part of her genetic heritage, her personality was validated with a new positive message. This freed her to move forward feeling satisfied with her unique set of traits and interests.

While children are born with unique personalities there is no question that nurture—the impact of the child's environment—tremendously affects the way personality develops. However, perception can be affected by new information and experience.

> *I was once chatting with a young man as he checked out my groceries at the market. He complained that he "always gets unfairly blamed for everything." I asked if he was a middle child. Surprised, he admitted he was. I explained that his complaint was one I often heard from middle children at the beginning of treatment. I suspected it was because of their early experiences with an older sibling who knew how to manipulate parental blame, and younger siblings who would get excused for their behaviors because they were younger. He decided to work with me as a client. During our sessions, he learned that he was no longer **just** a middle child. By encouraging him to look at his adulthood as having the power he lacked when he was child, he was able to rewrite the story and challenge what had proven to be a very limiting belief.*

Each of us has two parents. We all had to start from the joining of a sperm and an egg. Satir stressed the importance of this commonality we all share. She was always aware that whether the real parents were present or not, the "Ma, Pa, Kid" relationship was fundamental to the development of the "Kid's" sense of self. For that reason, she tried to provide a variety of ways for the "Kid" to heal his or her relationship with "Ma" and "Pa." The truth is that until that relationship finds peace, the "Kid" is generally looking for replacements—spouse, teacher, boss, etc.— that may or may not be an improvement on the original difficult family dynamic.

The Therapeutic Process

Therapists who choose to address the family system as a means of understanding current problems have a range of techniques they can apply. Whether all, part, or only one member of the family is present, it is still useful to understand the complaint within the context of the family of origin.

Satir entered a therapeutic environment using whichever technique or mode of entry (cognition, emotion, movement etc.) was most accessible. Once the client, or family, was engaged in the work, she gently invited them to use all their senses and processing skills to transform their perception of what was troubling them. The process of changing perception drove the transformation.

Configuration of the Therapy Session

Family Systems Therapy maintains that by changing the system in some way, or even just one individual in it, the entire dynamic of that system has to change. Family behavior is directly influenced by how each member perceives the others. My goal in family work is always to find the path into the system that will allow love, respect and mutual appreciation to grow. It is surprising how often that is the exact thing that all members long to experience.

> *Anita and Tom were ready to get a divorce. Both felt unappreciated and distant. I asked them each what one behavior would make them feel appreciated and reconnected. In Tom's case, it was cuddling at night before going to sleep. For Anita, it was having Tom listen to her talk about her day without trying to fix anything. I assigned them a 15 minute homework assignment where Anita could say whatever she needed to Tom (he would listen and empathize), while Anita cuddled and held Tom. After one week, they had rekindled their relationship and could focus on the real family crises, which revolved around stress from her job, as well as the children's learning challenges.*

Satir believed that feeling loved by our parents is a universal yearning. Most children start out eager to please their parents, and when they do, they feel lovable and capable. Notice how babies screech with joy, engaging with their parents' smiles and play. Toddlers and young children run to demonstrate new skills or to share their thoughts and experiences. Even as teenagers, when they are in the throes of seeking independence and differentiation, if the relationship with their parents is good, they still want approval—even as they make it challenging to give.

When children can't please their parents, or when their efforts are irregularly or randomly successful, their sense of self gets damaged. This can result in acting out, hurting or bullying others or themselves, withdrawal and despair. Experiments on monkeys deprived of their mother's love (they were given essentially milk-producing robots instead of mothers) yielded seriously mentally disturbed adult monkeys. The impact of a mother's touch and love cannot be underestimated. When a parent fails to give the child the consistent attention, love and care he or she craves, sometimes a mother figure or father figure such as a mentor or teacher can at least partially make up for the lack of parental affection.

Individuals who could not win their parents' approval may spend their lives searching for the love and confidence that these parents failed to impart. Often they look for that love from the same type of person—one who is unwilling or incapable of giving it. By re-creating a relationship that is comfortable in its familiarity, they are also often destined to continue the pattern of unfulfilled longing. This is one area where insight is the only way to break the pattern.

Therapist's Use of Self

Clients place their trust in the skill, integrity and person of the therapist. To be worthy of this trust, therapists must make every attempt to be congruent—say what they mean, with matching non-verbal cues, as well as modeling behaviors that reinforce what they've said.

As a therapist (and mother), I believe it is important to admit any biases or presuppositions I hold about parenting or behavior. I use the context of the family meeting, and the "new information" section, to disclose my most important rule: "Be Kind." Treating people with kindness includes showing attention and appreciation, and banning sarcasm, name-calling, physical harm or criticism. Children who are raised with kindness tend to feel more confident and to promote kindness in the world. Bullies result from being bullied.

> *Ten year-old Jolie was depressed and said that her only real motivation was to prove people wrong when they predicted she could or couldn't do something. Jolie's mother, Sue, described her own sadness and depression. Jolie's father, Burt, blamed all the family's problems on laziness and Sue's bad parenting. He refused to participate in the family therapy meetings because he wouldn't compliment, appreciate or acknowledge the positive things Jolie or her mother did. He couldn't think of anything positive to say about anyone. When asked to describe his own parents, Burt admitted they were a lot like him and Sue. When asked how that had turned out for him and his siblings, he began to cry.*

In extreme cases of abuse, children may develop alternate personalities. This defense mechanism compartmentalizes their painful experiences, removing them from conscious awareness. It allows them to cope with the pain they feel when someone who supposedly loves them resorts to physical, sexual, or emotional abuse. It doesn't matter to them how or why the parent became an abuser (even if it was because they too were abused.) For someone with Dissociative Identity Disorder (formerly called Multiple Personality Disorder), memories become hidden in the unconscious minds of different "parts" because to remember them all at once would be too painful. These old wounds require healing before the parts can reunite. For that to happen, one must be able to consciously address these experiences and to understand them in new ways that can positively change the message of the stories one takes into the future.

Family Sculpting

Satir often used a role-playing technique she created called Family Sculpting to illustrate family relationships and change beliefs. In family sculpting, the client (the Star) selects members of a group to represent family members (or ideas, ideals, or feelings.) The Star then coaches the "actors" in how to stand, look or speak in order to sufficiently represent their roles. When Satir was working with a client or family, she often had an audience available to play the necessary parts. The Star would select role-players and coach them on what they needed to represent. When there is no audience, it is possible to create stand-ins; puppets, clay figures, drawn diagrams, internet photos, or cartoon collector cards all work. The next goal of the Family Sculpture is to represent an "ideal" configuration of the family in a new sculpture. When the whole family is available for family work, each member can sculpt a "current" picture of the family, with the therapist standing in for the Star, and an "ideal" sculpt of the family. I often photograph each person's two representations; then we compare and analyze them. Whose pictures are similar? How are they different (perceptions or ideals are disparate)? What would it take to reach that ideal? Is it possible or desirable? Which members of the family would not like this ideal to become the new status quo?

Personal Stories

Much of who we are is contained in our story; our values, our dreams, our disappointments and fears are all alive in the story of our experiences and our feelings about them. While we may not remember every moment of our life, what we do remember colors everything. And sometimes that which we don't remember is the key to understanding our current reactions. This is one reason that psychotherapy begins with the person's story—it is their current truth. But it is not necessarily their final truth.

Sometimes we learn our story in our early life through our parents; they may teach us how to be, or how not to be. Parents often behave in ways that mimic what they experienced as children—unless they consciously choose different behaviors. And even if they want to be different, in times of stress, sometimes the old recording tape takes over.

> *A young mother called in tears because she'd gotten so frustrated with her arguing children she'd ended the conversation with the age-old "Do it because I said so..." "I've turned into my mother," she sighed. "Will it damage my children for life?"*

152 *Peace Within, Peace Between*

All of us have an internal tape of ideas, behaviors, responses, and values that our parents either professed, modeled, or both. Some were good—ones we appreciate and gladly teach the next generation; some were hurtful and damaging, or even immoral. We can only be responsible for our own behaviors and values. Hopefully, we live in integrity with what we teach our children. Even if we don't, it is always possible to change and improve the things that don't work well.

Illustrations

When the family (or client) is trying to understand old wounds, sometimes they can show a previous generation in a sculpture. In this case, the Star may not even have met some of the players, such as grandparents, parents who gave them up for adoption or deceased relatives. Satir would encourage them to make up details and to place the role-players as the Star imagines things looked in that family. The Star can ask questions, listen to the feelings of the role-players, and even tell them things that they wish they could have said in real life. Often just being able to speak the feelings or to hear what those people might have felt, can be healing. Plus, the role-player also seems to learn something about him- or herself from the experience of playing that role. In one case, a woman found herself frequently called upon to play the Ideal Mother. She gained a new appreciation for how much her nurturing nature affected the people she met.

> *Here are two sculpts by a 9 year-old boy (he selected photos from the internet to represent his family). In the "current" sculpt the Star left himself out entirely, and depicted the rest of the family as disconnected, walking in different directions, not noticing the beauty around them. His "ideal" sculpt shows the whole family together, holding hands, enjoying the scenery. He said his wish is to be closer to his father, and to have his mother and father get along better.*

Current Family   Ideal Family

Even if the "Kid" never knew a thing about the various parts in the sculpture, Satir would have the person make up a story about them. She did this, in part, to make them real, but also because the "Kid" always carried a story into his future, whether it was true or not. Often the story would turn out to be true, even though there was no conscious awareness of the facts. This demonstrates how powerful the story of our beginnings and past can be.

Each human being has a unique personal story—even identical twins have variations in their life experiences. They may have identical DNA and have been together virtually their whole life, but perception is person-specific, and we are all viewing the world through our own eyes, and applying a personal interpretation to every experience.

> ### *An Old Cherokee Tale of Two Wolves*
>
> *One evening an old Cherokee Indian told his grandson about a life battle that goes on inside people. He said, "My son, the battle is between two 'wolves' inside us all. One is Evil. It is anger, envy, jealousy, sorrow, regret, greed, arrogance, self-pity, guilt, resentment, inferiority, lies, false pride, superiority, and ego. The other is good. It is joy, peace, love, hope, serenity, humility, kindness, benevolence, empathy, generosity, truth, compassion and faith."*
> *The grandson thought quietly about the battle for a minute and then asked his grandfather: "Which wolf wins?"*
>
> *The old Cherokee simply replied, "The one you feed."* [2]

---

[2]Wizdompath Tales and Legends. (2012). Cherokee Tale of Two Wolves. (Retrieved September10, 2012 from http://wizdompath.wordpress.com/?s=cherokee)

Worksheet for Chapter 12: Parents and Others (Example)

Story: Describe the "story" of an area of conflict and what happened.

Old Thought/ Old Behavior: Describe the habitual thought or reaction you had.

New Thought/New Behavior: Describe a more positive thought and reaction.

Example:

Story: *It is Christmas morning and after opening his presents, Tommy starts to cry because he wanted a different video game.*

Old Thought: *"What an ungrateful child! How dare he cry after I got him all these gifts! I'll never give him another present again."*

Old Behavior: *Yelling your "old thoughts" at Tommy, and punishing him by taking back his other gifts.*

New Thought: *"How sad that I didn't manage to get Tommy the present he wanted when I was really trying. It is hard to be disappointed when you expected something else."*

New Behavior: *Acknowledging Tommy's disappointment; saying you are also disappointed that you guessed wrong about his presents. You were hoping he would like them. Suggesting three possible other solutions for him to choose between:*

1) Next year he should make a list of the gifts he wants most so you would have a better chance of getting him the most important one.

2) Giving him a gift card (and fast trip to the store) would be a better way to handle next Christmas.

3) They could take back the other presents he got and save up until he had enough credit to purchase the one he really wanted.

Worksheet for Chapter 12: Parents and Others

Story: Describe the "story" of an area of conflict and what happened.

Old Thought/ Old Behavior: Describe the habitual thought or reaction you had.

New Thought/New Behavior: Describe a more positive possible thought and reaction.

Try to imagine how other people involved might react differently to the New Behavior, as opposed to the Old Behavior.

Story:

Old Thought:

Old Behavior:

New Thought:

New Behavior:

Chapter Thirteen: Communication

"Communication is the largest single factor in determining what kinds of relationship one makes with others and what happens to each person in the world" – *Virginia Satir*

Facilitating Understanding

From the moment we are born (maybe even in utero) we use our senses to experience the world, and to understand and anticipate behavior in others. Even if we never speak a word, we are always communicating (both consciously and unconsciously) a wide range of information to others. Effective communication allows us to understand others, share feelings, clarify information, learn from experience, fulfill our dreams, build trust, and connect with others. Honest, open communication can aid us in our yearning to be authentic, accepted, valued, appreciated and loved. Communication is capable of smoothing or ruining all interactions. Healthy communication is essential when wanting to nurture, create and maintain intimacy.

A Recipe for Positive Communication

Virginia Satir's therapeutic model is often called a "Communication Model" because of the emphasis she placed on *how* we approach communication, particularly within families. Perhaps because she was deaf part of her childhood, she saw nonverbal factors, such as context, as being just as essential as the typical focus on content. How, when and why we communicate something (whether by words or actions) all have an effect on the outcome of the communication. At the heart of her model are considerations for effective, fulfilling, healthy communication, in short, the factors for positive communication.

Satir often spoke of triads or triangles in communication. In one, she identified three situational elements required for positive communication: *Timing, Appropriateness* and *Relevance* (TAR). TAR is an acronym to help you remember that failing to consider all three can turn any conversation into a "sticky wicket," if not an uncomfortable mess. In another, she described the "three-legged-stool" of content elements necessary for positive communication: *Other, Context*, and *Self (OCS)*. Without all three, communication is as tricky as a stool with a missing leg.

> *Recipe for Positive Communication*   Serves: Everyone
>
> *Ingredients of the **Situation***
> 1 Collaboration on **T**iming
> 3 Considerations of **A**ppropriateness
> 2 Thoughts on **R**elevance
>
> *Ingredients of the **Content***
> A Heaping scoop of **O**ther
> 2 Possibilities of **C**ontext
> 1 Sincere request of **S**elf
>
> Carefully prepare Situational Ingredients and set aside to gel. Plan and prepare each of your content ingredients individually. Do not mix. Add each Content Ingredient, in order, to prepared Situational Mix. Allow mixture to marinate before serving. Best if served with sincerity and warm intentions.

Considerations for Congruent Communication

Congruent communication occurs when one's words and actions match one's thoughts and values, and Other, Context and Self are all included. Satir considered congruent communication the only functional way of communicating.

The following communication considerations are designed to be effective, even under difficult circumstances. Incorporation of the six elements, three situational elements: TAR, three content elements: OCS, may not guarantee a positive outcome, but all are essential. Communication is unavoidably a mix of the current situation and factors from the past. The goal here is not to be academically complete but to provide a useable guide to effective positive communication.

Timing: Is This Person Available and Willing to Discuss the Issue?

Consideration of timing is important because it establishes a respectful basis for the communication. By asking *when* would be a good time for us to talk, we communicate several things: we acknowledge that the other person's time is as valuable to us as our own, that this is a conversation we intend to have, that we respect the other's needs, that we want the person's full attention, and that we are willing to wait until that attention is available. It also signals that we care about what is about to be discussed.

> ### Questions to Assess Timing
>
> - "Is this a good time to discuss…?"
> - "When would be a good time to talk about…?"
> - "Are you feeling well and rested enough to discuss…."

The first step in establishing a respectful connection is finding a mutually agreeable time so that the discussion has a chance of becoming a meeting of the minds. By essentially inviting the other person into the conversation, it is more likely they will be available to listen, potentially with an open heart, at the negotiated time. Sometimes, this is the single most important factor in getting the response we desire, particularly if we are requesting action of the other person.

Appropriateness: Is It Reasonable to Have This Discussion?

On one level, appropriateness is a reflection of whether what is communicated is appropriate in this context. A husband wants to discuss buying a larger house when the family is having trouble paying the current mortgage; a wife starts to discuss marital problems during a social evening with another couple; a parent wants to discuss her son's drug habit with one of his friends. Each of these situations is likely to result in a failed communication, even if every other ingredient is perfect.

Determining the appropriateness of a communication is a nuanced process occurring at numerous levels. I've provided focus questions in the chart below to guide you in navigating the complexity of appropriateness. While we cannot control how another person will react in any given interaction, we can and should understand our own feelings and motivations. If we want a positive outcome, and sometimes we don't (venting, revenge, etc.), we need to respect the circumstances and means we use in the communication.

Consider the appropriateness of the communication by asking, "Am I in a calm state?" "Is what I want to say being said to the right person, in an optimal environment, taking into consideration the emotional state and life circumstances of the other person?" If the answer is "no" to any of these aspects, it might be a good idea to go back to the drawing board. There are, of course, urgent circumstances where we can't wait for a stressless environment, but even then, self-awareness and insight are the necessary foundation of a positive communication. The goal of positive communication is to "act" instead of "react," so that we are building trust and confidence in the relationship (whatever its nature) going forward.

Questions to Ask About Appropriateness

What? Is the topic of discussion appropriate in this situation?

- Do I know everything I need to know about the larger situation?
- Is this situation related to a past wound in myself that should be addressed first?
- Is it possible to discuss this situation without bringing in the past?
- Am I clear about what I need and am asking for in this discussion?
- Has a recent event made this discussion inappropriate?

Who? Is this the right person for this discussion?

- Is my reaction really about this person or someone from my past?
- Is the person interested in what I want to discuss?
- Does he or she have the power or desire to do anything about the situation?
- Does he or she know anything about it that could add to my understanding?
- Is there a relationship or responsibility that would make it difficult for the person to speak freely?
- Does the person have the skills or compassion that will give me a helpful response?

Where? Is this the best place to have this discussion?

- Is it private—sufficiently quiet and free of distractions?
- Do other people who are present need or want to be there?
- Are other activities (such as eating or socializing) going to disturb the communication?

When? Is this the right time to have this discussion?

- Am I emotionally ready to discuss this?
- Would it be better to wait until feelings calm down?
- Is there enough time available to complete the discussion?
- Is this time appropriate when considering current events in both our lives?

How? ….Continued on next page…

> **Appropriateness Questions** (continued)
>
> *How?* *Is this the way I want to discuss this?*
>
> - Do I really want a discussion or do I just want to vent my feelings?
> - Is this the best way to approach the situation?
> - Can I ask questions that will better clarify the situation?
> - Are my reactions and feelings out of proportion to this situation?
> - Is it possible to be sensitive of needs of Other/Context/Self when I feel this way?

***Relevance**: Is This Communication Connected to the Current Situation?*

Relevance is defined as having a logical connection to the matter being discussed. In communication that means sticking to the current subject, solution or process. While it may *seem* relevant to bring up the past or related behaviors that appear connected to this current topic, it is only useful if this particular discussion will be helped by adding this information. If the information is relevant, it will add to the conversation. If it isn't relevant, it can evoke emotions that can side track or end the conversation.

> *Cora had a terrible habit of starting a conversation with someone without considering any of the elements that facilitate good communication. She might enter a conversation already in progress (timing), interrupt aggressively (appropriateness), and begin discussing something only she cared about (relevance). People soon learned to avoid her, if at all possible, and left a conversation as soon as she entered it, knowing that she was unlikely to communicate anything that would interest them, and worse, she would do it in an offensive way.*

> **Questions to Assess the Relevance of a Topic**
>
> - Is this topic about the current situation?
> - Does understanding the history of the topic help or hurt going forward?
> - Is this a generalization about past events, instead of focusing on now?
> - Is this a new topic or one that relates to the current discussion?
> - Is this subject of interest, or significant to this person at this time?

Acknowledging the "Other"

While the situational elements are essential to managing the context for positive communication, it is the content elements that provide the heart power of congruent communications. In my experience, acknowledging "other" might be the single most helpful component of a successful communication strategy. When we begin a communication with an accurate acknowledgement of what the other person, the listener, might be feeling or thinking, we open their heart to hearing what we might want or need. This occurs because we have begun the discussion by validating what the other person needs in this situation. It takes compassion to understand what the other person might be feeling or needing. Finding positive intention in the "other" is essential for beginning congruent, respectful communication. It is often effective to combine the acknowledgment with the invitation to the conversation described under timing. The effect in both cases is to create a heart opening.

Questions to Begin a Communication by Acknowledging the "Other"

What might the listener be feeling about this topic of discussion?

- "My guess is that you feel _____ about _____..."
- "Do you feel _____ about _____...?"
- "I know you might be feeling _____..."

What might the listener be thinking about this topic of discussion?

- "You've probably already thought about _____..."
- "You might have already considered _____ and _____..."
- "I understand you've already put a lot of thought into this…"

What might the listener want or need from this topic of discussion?

- "It seems like you might want _____..."
- "I'm thinking you would like _____..."
- "I hear that what you want/need in this situation is _____..."

If you have guessed wrong on any of the above, this type of beginning can be used to create an opening. Thank the person for correcting you. Convey that you really *want* to acknowledge what the other person thinks, feels, wants or needs and you are really glad you checked these factors out before continuing. The intent is to establish and express sincere compassion of your thoughts and feelings. Without our sincerity and compassion this strategy reduces the communication to formulaic manipulation.

Acknowledging the "Context"

The second important element of congruent communication is an acknowledgment of what the *situation* might require under the current circumstances. Satir called this the Context and by stating it second in the conversation, we establish criteria for judging the request that is embedded in the last part of the communication, the "Self" component.

The Context describes what is necessary to be successful in the particular circumstances, without the emotional considerations of what either person wants or needs in this situation.

Questions to Recognize the Context of a Communication

- What does the situation **need** to be successful?
   "In this situation, we need to be/do/have/complete …"

- What are the **goals** of the situation?
   "Whatever we decide, the goal of all this is …"

- What are the important **requirements** in this situation, separate from the needs of the people involved?
   "Apart from what either of us wants in this situation, we need to consider …"

- What **facts** are immutable in this situation?
   "Regardless of what either of us would prefer, we can't change the fact that …"

- If an objective observer were to analyze the situation, what **vital elements** would be emphasized?
   "Any outsider would immediately accept that …"

Asking for What You Want or Need - the "Self"

For some of us, knowing and being able to ask for what we want or need is very difficult. We might have learned that we didn't deserve to get what we wanted, or that asking for it was bad or selfish. Or, we might be so focused on the good of the organization or making other people happy that we sublimate what we want. For others, getting what we want is the most important part of their communication.

Obviously, this part of the communication is worth considering and planning. If we don't ask for what we want, it is unlikely we will get it. In general, the best communications include a concrete, observable request that is clearly stated and is a logical outcome of the previous elements, the Other and the Context.

Questions for the "Self" Statement

1) What do you **want** as an outcome of this conversation?
   "What I would like to see is _____"

2) Is there something you **need** from this conversation?
   "Going forward, I really need _____"

3) Do you have **feelings** to express or to be considered after this conversation?
   "In the future, please consider my sensitivity to _____"
   "I feel _____ when _____ and I would prefer to feel _____ in the future."
   "If you would _____, I wouldn't feel so _____ next time."

While there is no guarantee that the listener will agree to what you ask, asking this way exponentially increases the likelihood that you will have a better connection going forward, even if more discussion is necessary to reach an agreement.

Other Components of Communication

There are other elements of communication that affect how our communications are received and if they will be effective. Some are not verbal, such as tone of voice, facial expression, and body stance. These can communicate information to the listener that might not even be conscious. Every aspect of the communication, especially the nonverbal ones, communicate something to the listener, and are capable of eliciting a strong emotional response.

Students in a communication class were asked to pair with a complete stranger for an exercise. Without speaking, they were asked to write a paragraph on what they knew and felt about the person—just from looking at the partner. When they finished writing, they shared their "impressions" with the group. Everyone described an array of feelings, personality traits and opinions about their partner. Few, however, were accurate; most represented the unconscious associations the students made with someone they knew who looked or dressed like their partner.

Learning Style and Communication

Learning style also plays a role in the effectiveness of the communication. Auditory-sequential learners are usually facile with words; yet they tend to explain things directly and succinctly. They may have difficulty understanding when someone is describing a picture. Visual-spatial learners might not tune in to the verbal communication, getting more information from the nonverbal cues (e.g., facial expression, body stance, etc.). In addition, they may over-explain, restate an idea several different ways, or make tangential associations to make a point. Tactile-kinesthetic learners might only be able to listen when they are doing something or moving, giving the impression that they are not listening at all. An additional factor to take into account is thinking versus feeling types. Individuals who are highly emotional might become flooded when the conversation becomes charged with feelings. For communication to be optimal, the listener's learning style and personality style should be considered, to whatever extent possible.

Being Right or Not Being Wrong

One of the barriers to connecting is that many people need to "be right" or "not be wrong" more than they need to find connection. When a communication is perceived in that light, there is usually resistance to being able to empathize or validate the other person's feelings. A big impediment to positive communication can be mismatched developmental ages of the speakers. When an adult is stuck at a younger emotional age, it generally takes a talented facilitator to overcome immature communication patterns in "being right" or "not wrong."

Another aspect of the "being right/not being wrong" response has to do with old experiences and meanings made about them. Being told we are wrong, when we feel that we are right, elicits a strong negative response, and may trigger emotional wounds from our family of origin. For intuitive types who have grown up with sensing types (see Chapter 8 on Personality Types), this can be particularly painful since they cannot "prove" or show the source of their knowledge. One way to avoid triggering old wounds in others is to qualify our statements, saying things like, "Hmmm, I didn't think that was true, but I could be mistaken," or "I didn't hear that, but anything is possible."

The Effective Apology

While on the subject of overcoming triggered reactions and hurt feelings, the most important, yet often misunderstood attempt at reconnection is the apology. For some people, it is the most difficult human interaction to accomplish successfully; for others, it is difficult because they equate it with admitting fault or bad behavior (neither of which they feel is deserved.)

> ### Example of an Unproductive Apology
>
> Jenny: "You left your dishes in the sink and now ants are everywhere."
> Joe: "I'm sorry, but you always do, too."

Most of the time, anger is an expression of hurt and disappointment. So when there is an opportunity to apologize, it is important to focus on the underlying feelings. The event itself may be forgotten, but the feelings behind it could last forever. Preserving the relationship and building connection should be the goal of a productive apology.

In the example above, Jenny is still angry even though she got an apology. Why? Jenny is frustrated that she has a sink full of ants. She probably has made a meaning about the behavior, such as "You don't care about me" or "You think I'm your slave." The apology does not indicate that anything will be different in the future, and justifies his behavior.

Including the "Other/Context/Self" formula isn't the only thing that makes an apology effective. What is not said can be as important as what is. Several omissions make an apology more likely to be a success: no excuse, reason or justification is offered for why the offense occurred; there is no suggestion that the other person is overreacting or not entitled to his or her feelings; there is no reference to past times the person did the same or similar things; there is no list of behaviors that should offset this one. Perhaps, most significant, there is no attempt to blame the other person for one's mistake. If strengthening the connection and healing the injury is the goal, stick to the basic effective apology. Remember that the goal of the apology is to make amends for hurting the other person, and to help the person know that you didn't intend to hurt him or her.

> **Example of an Effective or Reconnecting Apology**
>
> 1) Admit what you did and validate the other person's feelings (Other).
>   "*I'm sorry I* left the dishes out and ants are everywhere; it wasn't my intention to upset you, and I can understand how that would."
>
> 2) State how you will fix it, if you can (Context).
>   "*I would be happy to* clean them and get rid of the ants immediately."
>
> 3) State what you will do differently in the future so this won't happen again (Context).
>   "*In the future I will* clean up after myself as soon as I'm done eating."
>
> 4) Admit your feelings and wishes (Self).
>   "*I feel sad that I* upset you. I would really like to make this up to you. What can I do?"

Discussing Problems

Eventually, even the most congenial and compatible relationships need some discussion of differences. Discussing any problem follows the same model of the Other/Context/Self (OCS) formula, after Timing/Appropriateness/Relevance (TAR) considerations have been addressed.

> **Questions to Ask Before Initiating a Difficult Discussion**
>
> - Is this a battle worth waging?
> - Is this something that will not go away unless addressed?
> - Am I in a good place (healthy, alert etc.) to judge and discuss the problem?
> - What are some possible solutions to the problem?

This simple script demonstrates the elements necessary for an effective discussion:

Discussion Script

(Other) **I understand you might** (*fill in possible reason for behavior*)
(e.g., not have noticed/ have been distracted/ have had different priorities, etc.)

(Context) **And, when** (*state the fact of the event*) **happens/ed/,**

(Self) **I feel/ felt** (*fill in feelings*).
(e.g., *fear, hurt, disappointed, angry etc.*)

(Self) **My wish/hope is that next time** (*state a different way that the person might act or respond*).

Example: *"I understand you felt justified when you yelled at me yesterday; it hurt my feelings; in the future, please quietly and privately tell me what you'd like me to do differently."*

An old joke captures some of the challenges implicit in communication:

> *The inmates on a prison block had been there so long that instead of telling the same old jokes, they'd numbered them and, every once in a while, someone would yell out the appropriate number, to which everyone would laugh.*
>
> *One day, Avery yelled out "34." Silence followed.*
>
> *So he yelled it out again "34." More silence.*
>
> *"Why isn't anyone laughing at 34? Usually everyone loves that joke." Avery yelled.*
>
> *"You told it wrong."*

Communication is always more than just a transfer of words. It has the potential to help us learn about ourselves and others as well as building (or destroying) connections. As long as we want to connect with others, it is in our best interest to find the best possible way to share thoughts, feelings, and words that create intimacy, and express our deepest needs, vulnerabilities and dreams.

Worksheet #1 for Chapter 13: Communication

Activity: Practice creating Other, Context and Self statements for something you would like to discuss using the Discussion Script below as a Guideline.

Discussion Script
(Other) **I understand you might** (*fill in possible reason for behavior*)
(e.g., not have noticed/ have been distracted/ have had different priorities, etc.)

(Context) **And, when** (*state the fact of the event*) happens/ed/,

(Self) **I feel/ felt** (*fill in feelings*).
(e.g., fear, hurt, disappointed, angry etc.*)*

(Self) **My wish/hope is that next time** (*state a different way that the person might act or respond*).

Item to be Discussed:_____

_____

Other Statement:_____

_____

_____

Context Statement:_____

_____

_____

Self Statement:_____

_____

_____

_____

Worksheet #2 for Chapter 13: Communication

Effective or Reconnecting Apology

Activity: Create an Effective Apology using Other, Context and Self statements for a situation in which an apology would help repair a relationship.

Example Script:

1) **Admit what you did and validate the person's feelings** (Other).
   "I'm sorry I left the dishes out and ants are everywhere; it wasn't my intention to upset you, and I can understand how that would."

2) **State how you will fix it, if you can** (Context).
   "I would be happy to clean them and get rid of the ants immediately."

3) **State what you will do differently in the future so this it won't happen again** (Context).
   "In the future I will clean up after myself as soon as I'm done eating."

4) **Admit your feelings of regret and wishes for going forward** (Self).
   "I feel sad that I upset you. I would really like to make this up to you. What can I do?"

Event or action needing apology: _____
_____
_____

Other Statement: _____
_____
_____

Context Statement: _____
_____
_____

Self Statement: _____
_____
_____

Chapter Fourteen: The Tip of the Iceberg

"Life is not what it's supposed to be. It's what it is. The way you cope with it is what makes the difference."
– Virginia Satir

Behavior, Coping Stances, and Defenses

Virginia Satir wisely evaluated individuals both in their beautiful uniqueness and in the context of their family and life interactions. Each of us is a complex combination of our personal qualities and our environmental influences. Our behaviors and how we interpret the world are all related to what we learned in our families of origin. Satir understood that in families we absorb messages that later surface in how we relate to the world. Each factor that changes how we perceive and react to our world has the potential to change an outcome of an interaction—for good or ill. For this reason alone, it is important to understand the mechanisms we've developed to better navigate our past, and that have the potential to improve our futures.

We develop survival strategies, coping stances, when we are very young. We apply them in times of stress and we use defense mechanisms to protect our vulnerable feelings. Our perceptions of what is happening are colored by what we have learned, and we assign "meanings" to what we perceive in an attempt to understand our world.

This chapter examines the coping stance layer of Satir's Iceberg Model. Satir was very visual. Her graphic metaphor gives a sense of how she *saw* behavior in a way that words alone cannot convey. Satir's Iceberg Model (See illustration below) is a representation of how so much of what drives our feelings and behaviors happens inside of us, much of it below the level of our consciousness. This model is very dense, and could be a book in itself. I will primarily address the tip of the iceberg here, the behaviors the world sees—how we present ourselves to others. The other layers are described briefly to provide context.

Above the Waterline: Behavior and Its Possibilities

Behavior is what we do or say that is visible to the world. It comes from a complex and often instantaneous set of interactions that occur below the waterline. Below the waterline we find our feelings (about what happened); our feelings about those feelings (if they are acceptable to us); our perceptions (about what our senses tell us has happened and what meaning we ascribe to them); our expectations (what we think should have happened); our yearnings and

Virginia Satir's Personal Iceberg Model

Behavior
(What the world sees and hears, the story)

Coping Stances
(Blaming, Placating, Distracting, Computer, Stonewalling, Congruent)

Feelings
(Happiness, hurt, fear, sadness, anger, excitement, etc.)

Feelings about Feelings
(Judgments, values, rules about our feelings)

Perceptions
(Our subjective reality, meanings, thoughts, assumptions, beliefs, ideas, values)

Expectations
(What we feel or think will or should happen)

Yearnings (Universal)
(To feel connected, free, purposeful, validated, loved and lovable)

Longings (Person Specific)
(Your personal wishes, dreams, goals)

Self ("I Am")
(Core being, life-force, spirit, essence, soul)

longings (what our hearts want); and our inner Self (core values and intrinsic personality traits). Feelings and perceptions both connect closely to the real visible world above the waterline. Emotionally, behavior rests primarily on feelings. Physiologically, perceptions link the physical world to the feelings below, and in some models appear higher on the iceberg. Both representations are apt. In other interactions, expectations, yearnings and Self may float closer to the top. Some Satir practitioners place expectations above perception on the Iceberg. A good case can be made either way. Since perceptions are based on beliefs, values, and past images, expectations could flow from what we have internalized from our past, and the meanings would be a result of expectations, accurate or not. At the same time, our perceptions are colored by our expectations, which also can come from a range of experience and learned rules. In either case, our feelings are a result of this process.

Each of the submerged levels symbolizes a product from a lifetime of experience. But the experience that serves as the foundation for our understanding of reality is not set in stone. A shift in our perceptions inevitably alters our feelings, expectations, and our sense of Self. When we ascribe a different meaning to a life-shaping event, this new awareness changes our life experience, and enables us to move in a new direction. The process of transforming our lives to fulfill our dreams involves understanding what is, then analyzing if something different would be better. Until we breathe our last breath, change is possible.

Virginia Satir's Coping Stances

Coping Stances are the behaviors we use unconsciously at times of stress and conflict. We learn them at an early age, when we are the most vulnerable, to help us survive our childhood. Most of us learn both useful and dysfunctional survival strategies. Once we adopt certain coping strategies that appeared to work in our family of origin, we tend to rely on these for the rest of our lives, as fallback measures whenever we feel threatened. A particular coping strategy may or may not be useful in the long run. A two year-old might be forgiven for a temper tantrum; a 50 year-old man usually isn't.

Most of us fine-tune our coping strategies over time, based upon the reactions we evoke with them. We find more effective ways of behaving in our daily lives; however, under stress, or when back in our family of origin (or a similar system, such as our marriage or a particular work setting), most people unconsciously revert to old ways of coping. Satir sought a pathway to the development of new, more effective coping strategies. She found the solution in the addition of behavioral elements to existing coping stances to create congruent behavior. By using *Congruent* coping strategies, we are far more likely to build and maintain satisfying relationships.

A Functional Coping Stance: Congruent

A Congruent coping stance incorporates the three context elements of communication: the Other, the Context, and the Self (OCS). Particularly in times of conflict or disagreement people have difficulty achieving a satisfying outcome without all three. When we act in ways that are congruent with what we say and think—and consider the feelings of the **Other** people involved, the needs of the situation or **Context** *and* what we (**Self**) are feeling, people usually respond with more compassion and reason.

The *Congruent* Coping Stance

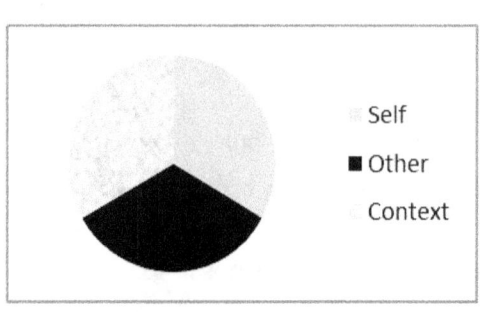 

Incorporates the *Other*, the *Context*, and the *Self*

In a *Congruent* coping response, words, body language, tone of voice, facial expression and inner feelings all match. When we are being congruent, we ask questions to clarify and acknowledge the feelings and desires of the *Other* people involved. We discuss and explore the needs of the situation—the *Context*. We make requests, or express honestly what we (the *Self*) are feeling and would like to see happen as a result of the discussion. When we are being congruent, we listen, ask questions, and express thoughts and feelings in a respectful way—making eye contact, staying calm. We may restate what we hear to make sure we have an accurate understanding of the other person's wishes and needs. We attend to the circumstances and requirements of the situation. In congruent interactions, we express our opinions, feelings, wants and needs in a respectful way, listen to what the other person wants to say, and consider the facts so that mutual understanding and connection is more. We may suggest solutions that are creative, unique, and competent, and that consider all the factors that are co-existing and relevant. The inner experience of a congruent person is self-awareness, relatedness, self-respect, competence, curiosity, harmony, and self-esteem. This is the goal of Satir-based therapy.

Dysfunctional Coping Stances

Satir observed that, for each individual, a few specific coping stances appeared to be used over and over again, regardless of the circumstance. Subtle deficiencies in some left them dysfunctional, always damaging the connection between people and limiting communication.

Satir originally presented four dysfunctional coping stances: *Placating, Blaming, Irrelevant, and Super-reasonable*. Later, the name *Computer* was used interchangeably with *Super-reasonable*, and Irrelevant became *Distractor*, to better describe the behavior of the stance. Still later, Satir's colleagues added another coping stance, *Stonewalling*, to describe someone who stops or leaves the discussion. Identifying dysfunctional coping stances in our practices and converting them to congruent responses is probably the most powerful way to promote happier and healthier relationships with ourselves and with others.

The Placating Coping Stance

Only Considers *Other*

When we adopt the **Placating** *coping stance,* we ignore our needs and feelings (*Self*) as well as the requirements of the situation (*Context*) to focus on the needs of *Other* people—wanting to please them, or to avoid conflict, regardless of the costs. Satir identified several variations of placators:

Explicit placators may beg, apologize, excuse, whine, or just agree, regardless of how they feel or what they want, or what the situation requires. ***Strategic placators*** may say one thing and do another, later trying to surreptitiously regain their power through passive-aggressive behavior or getting revenge. ***Chronic placators*** are trapped into routinely applying this stance in even the most benign conflicts, and consequently may become depressed or suicidal since they seldom see hope of ever getting their needs met.

We learn to placate when, as children, we ask for something we want or need and are punished, or made to feel shame or guilt just for asking. If love and approval were only given for compliance or self-sacrifice, we also learn to associate love with making concessions, and loss-of-love with asking for what we want.

Placators would rather do without than ask for what they want. When they do ask, it is only for things they really need. If they are refused those requests, they may stop asking, and can end up feeling despair or anger. Even in the best of circumstances, placators tend to feel helpless, resentful and have low self-worth. Sometimes placators have physical problems that stem from not expressing feelings or getting needs met, such as immune system deficiencies, muscle aches, headaches, or even cancer. Sometimes accused of being martyrs or dependent, they try to be "perfect" by ignoring or denying their own needs.

The Blaming Coping Stance

Only Considers *Self*

Those who adopt the ***Blaming*** stance have a strong investment in being "right" or at least "**not** being wrong." Blamers are created in very punitive environments where parents think in terms of black and white, without considering circumstances or intention. When using a Blaming coping stance, individuals generally do not take responsibility for their behavior. Some seem to keep a scoreboard of wrongs to place their "opponent" at a disadvantage. They don't take into account *Other* people's feelings or intentions, nor the circumstances (*Context*)—focusing only on what they want to get or what they think they need. Often they are perceived as bullies since they don't consider the other person's feelings, and usually get their way by using fear and intimidation. In the short term, they feel powerful and satisfied, as if they "won." They will often ask for anything they want, whenever they want it, because that is their only focus.

What Blamers don't realize is that their blaming behavior builds resentment in the people they discount. Blamers might feel lonely and paranoid (accurately, since people often do try to get back at them in the long run). Blaming behavior is usually judgmental, dictatorial and critical; blamers often feel angry, resentful, and vengeful. Their inner tension may express itself physically as high blood pressure, heart disease or stroke, constipation, muscle tension or back pain. While Blamers may be feared or given a wide berth, they are generally not respected or liked, because they are disrespectful in the way they treat others.

Chapter Fourteen: The Tip of the Iceberg   181

The Super-Reasonable (Computer) Coping Stance

Only Considers *Context* or Facts

People who act **Super-reasonable** (like a computer) tend to value logic and analysis over feelings. They are often bright, eloquent and able to "prove" the wisdom of whatever position they select. They feel that a cool, calm and collected discussion can lead to "reasonable" and "rational" decisions. Their posture (both literal and figurative) is rigid, and they rely on verbal manipulation, compulsion, rationalized acts and principles to back up rules and values.

The Super-reasonable often do not maintain eye contact or engage in reciprocal discussions. Instead, they tend to give lectures using abstract words and long patronizing explanations or analyses—sometimes acting arrogant and superior. They can be obsessive-compulsive, isolated, lonely, or unable to express feelings or feel compassion for others. They can be socially awkward and withdrawn. Because they are often oblivious to their own needs and feelings (*Self*), they usually don't get them met. By focusing on the needs of the situation, they ignore the needs of *Others*. Their relationships are usually difficult and unsatisfying because, in every conflict, no one ends up feeling valued or heard.

The Irrelevant (Distractor) Coping Stance

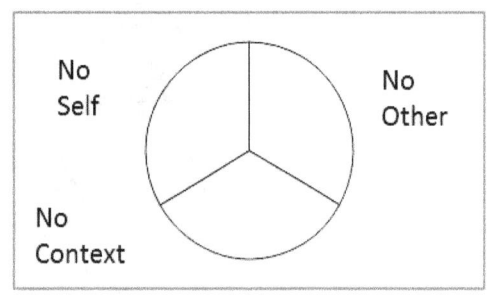

Ignores *Other, Context* and *Self*

Those who use the ***Irrelevant*** (or ***Distractor***) coping stance avoid conflict by distracting people from the source of the conflict. In children we often see this when parents start to argue; the child will do anything to distract them—break something, provoke a sibling, make too much noise, demand attention or change the subject. The child would rather get into trouble than live with the unbearable anxiety of experiencing the parents' conflict. As adults, distractors may ask tangential questions, tell jokes, change the subject or avoid making a point to distract from the anxiety-producing topic being discussed. Everyone leaves these discussions or meetings frustrated and confused as the difficult discussion stagnates in distraction and gets postponed.

Distractors often seem fidgety or hyperactive; they can be like a butterfly in motion—moving from subject to subject, interrupting anyone trying to stay on track. Their inner experience is feeling inconsequential, that "nobody cares if I don't make a scene." When distracting they may feel insecure, out of balance, overwhelmed, and that they don't fit anywhere. They may be socially awkward and have trouble sustaining attention, jobs and relationships.

Their inner experience may be one of confusion, frustration, incompetence or stupidity. Their inner disorientation may show up as stomach related dis-ease (nausea, constipation) or involve the central nervous system such as AD/HD, migraine headaches, pinched nerves, or strained muscles. People may find them initially entertaining, but quickly get frustrated by their inability to focus and be serious about decisions and repairing conflict.

Chapter Fourteen: The Tip of the Iceberg 183

Stonewalling Coping Stance

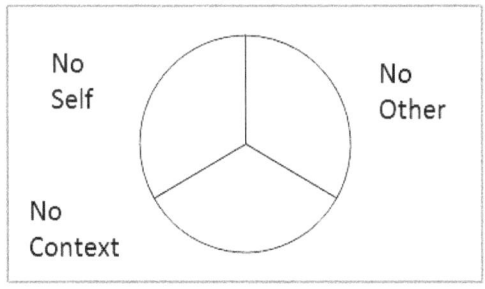

Ends Communication By Creating A Wall Between *Other* and *Self*

The coping stance **Stonewalling** was added to Satir's model because, in times of conflict, some people erect a wall or remove themselves from relating to others. They may hide (literally) or leave precipitously rather than face the possibility of hurting the relationship or themselves. Frequently, they are so overwhelmed or flooded with strong feelings that they just shut down. Conflict may cause them to feel confused, ineloquent, or to fear embarrassment. Some fear that any response will hurt others, either physically or emotionally, or will lead to their being hurt.

Stonewallers may have mixed feelings: relief that they avoided the problem; frustration and disappointment that they were unable to ask for what we wanted or to express their feelings; loneliness since they lost an opportunity to strengthen the relationship (or potentially ended the relationship altogether). Feeling inadequate, they may repress both their memories of unpleasant interactions and the feelings elicited by those experiences.

Because Stonewallers are essentially using the same "discount everyone and everything" process as the Distractor, their physical reactions would be similar: feeling shut down, constipated, have breathing disorders like asthma, stomach problems or headaches. With Stonewalling, both the other person and the Stonewaller usually feel frustrated, angry, hurt and depressed. They usually feel unsatisfied by not being able to clear the air or discuss the situation. It isn't a bad idea to ask for a time-out when feeling overwhelmed, Stonewalling, however, is leaving the conversation without the intention of a follow-up.

Changing a Dysfunctional Coping Stance

Old habits are hard to break. A lifetime of placating or distracting makes us wonderfully effective at it. But once we decide to improve our relationships and communication, we can choose to learn, practice and adopt congruent behavior. We add an option, and use it when we need it.

Adding Congruent Skills to your Coping Strategies

1) Identify your primary and secondary dysfunctional coping stance:
   Blaming, Placating, Computer, Distracting, Stonewalling
   Practice an exaggerated version of your natural coping stances.

2) Practice the skills of Congruent Coping
   Identify congruent non-verbal skills:
   Good eye contact, relaxed body stance, voice calm in tone, pace and volume.
   Express compassion for the **Other** person's feelings, needs, wants.
   Ask for clarifying information about the **Other** person's perspective and the **Context**.

3) Clearly state what you see as the needs of the situation, the **Context**.
   Identify what you (your **Self**) need in this situation.
   Respectfully and clearly ask for what you need or want from this situation.

Remember, our coping stances are default survival strategies when we feel overwhelmingly threatened or vulnerable. Once we have practiced the skills needed to be congruent, we can choose to use them or our default stance. Generally, congruent behavior makes other people feel less threatened and releases them from needing to use their own dysfunctional coping stance. It is far easier to stay congruent when one isn't reacting to someone else blaming, distracting, computing or placating.

When we have all the information that is available, we are far more likely to stay congruent; this is why asking questions is a good way to begin a congruent interaction. As with any skill, practice makes it easier to stay congruent instead of being washed away in the wave of fears that you won't get your needs considered, won't solve the problem or will damage the relationship.

> **Sample Questions That Might Elicit Congruent Behavior in Others**
>
> - How can we make a decision that takes into account what we both want, **and** what the situation requires?
> - What do you want to see happen in this situation?
> - Would it be possible for both of us to get part of what we want? Under these circumstances, could we postpone doing something until we agree on the best plan?
> - Is there a compromise position that would be "good enough?"

Defense Mechanisms

Part of the persistence of natural coping stances is their reflection of defense mechanisms. By understanding the mechanics of defense we get leverage for deactivating the coping stances they fuel.

Human beings are programmed to survive threat. Whether that threat is a saber-toothed tiger or an angry wife, our bodies are provided with the chemicals that help us react quickly in the interest of self-preservation. That mechanism is called the "fight or flight" reflex. In some circumstances, the threat may be tangible, such as a threat of physical violence; in other cases, something may be *perceived* as threatening to self-esteem or to one's work, family or social system. In any threat, people have several mechanisms that can protect them. In the face of physical threat, the fastest runner or the most skillful archer may have the advantage (providing they have a safe place to run, or a bow and arrows). But for an emotional threat, such as one that may undermine self-esteem, or create loss of status in the eyes of someone important, defense mechanisms provide us with protection for our ego.

Satir identified three primary defenses we use to handle feelings from emotional threats: denying (claiming the feeling doesn't exist at all); ignoring (knowing some feeling is there, but refusing to see it); and projecting (mistakenly seeing our own feelings in the motivations of others). Satir considered acceptance an additional defense mechanism; I personally believe however that acceptance signals readiness to move on past a defensive reaction. While defenses are mainly unconscious processes—we don't decide to deny something happened—they translate into observable reactions, so they straddle the waterline in Satir's Iceberg Model. These defenses are useful when we feel threatened, but they often prevent us from growing stronger in ourselves and our relationships.

Denial

As human beings, there are infinite ways we can apply the defense mechanisms that protect the "Self" from emotional damage. Denial is unconsciously deciding to forget something ever happened.

> *Bruce liked to get drunk at parties and regularly drove home after several drinks. After his third drunk driving conviction, his license was suspended. "Just bad luck," he claimed. He lost his job after missing too many Monday mornings nursing a hangover. "My boss never liked me," he explained. He insisted he wasn't an alcoholic because he could stop drinking whenever he wanted, and just liked to drink socially. When his wife left him, he had to face the fact that his life was being ruined by his alcoholism and he had been in denial about it.*

The most extreme form of denial is complete dissociation or creating alternate parts or personalities to employ when threatened (Dissociative Identity Disorder, previously called Multiple Personality Disorder[3]). These alternate parts may not "remember" the feeling or experience at all. In cases of deep trauma, people can develop alternate selves who essentially deal with difficult feelings so the full Self can avoid them altogether, and still function in the world as if nothing happened. Most of us are able to eventually "forget" unpleasant experiences, or to relegate them to the past for most of our conscious lives. But these old wounds still exist in our subconscious. As described in previous chapters, when a similar painful experience re-opens the wound, the reaction can be extreme, or just out of proportion to the current experience.

Ignoring What We See and/or Feel

When we know something exists, but choose to believe it doesn't apply to us, we find a way to ignore the facts. Rationalization, where we find logical reasons to excuse behavior, facilitates this process. Over time, however, using this defense mechanism will undermine trust and credibility.

> *Rosa was married to Eli for fifty nine years. Eli loved women and had been unfaithful to Rosa their whole marriage, but only with women in different cities and of a different religion. Rosa ignored the infidelity because she saw no direct evidence of it and wanted to stay married to Eli. Eli rationalized that "what Rosa didn't know didn't hurt her." Both had to ignore the infidelity so they could retain their self-esteem and the marriage.*

---

[3] American Psychiatric Association. (2000). *Diagnostic and statistical manual of mental disorders* (4th ed., text rev.). Washington, DC.

Projection

Projection is a more devious defense mechanism. In projection, the person is aware of the painful feelings, but protects their sense of Self by projecting their own negative feelings onto others. An extreme example is the legal case of Jane Roe, the famous test of abortion rights. Jane Roe sued the Supreme Court for the right to end her pregnancy. In a landmark decision (that is still being challenged), the court allowed her to end the pregnancy by declaring abortion lawful. We can only guess the complexity of her guilt over the abortion, because she later became a highly vocal opponent of abortion rights, projecting her personal guilt onto women contemplating or getting an abortion. Another form of projection occurs when a person accuses another of feeling or doing what they themselves feel, or do, such as the cheating husband who accuses his wife of infidelity.

> *Coretta, a distracted, anxious and strict mother, had toddler boys who adored their Aunt Loretta, who was more relaxed, loving and attentive. After a mix-up about the day Loretta was going to pick them up at the airport, Coretta flew into a rage, accusing Loretta of purposefully stranding them, and trying to hurt her and her children. In fact, these and other negative emotions were projected feelings that Coretta felt towards her sister. By projecting her own feelings onto Loretta, Coretta felt justified in ending her boys' contact with their aunt.*

Acceptance

When we accept our feelings and learn something from them, we grow stronger, healthier relationships—within ourselves and with others. Kübler-Ross[4] identified five stages of grief and loss: acceptance was the final stage—the one that signaled readiness and ability to move on with life. Satir conceptualized acceptance as a defense mechanism, which suggests that she saw it as another tool for the toolbox. I consider acceptance a tool to bring us to a new starting point so that we can regain enough equilibrium to begin again.

When we are ready to grow, we can choose a better tool to get what we want and need. Satir never expected or encouraged people to just stop old habits; she encouraged them to consider new possibilities. Substituting a better defense mechanism or coping strategy is a process. Practicing and then experimenting with new ways of being and reacting gradually reinforces new behaviors. The positive responses we get motivate us to want to apply the new strategies more often.

---

[4] Kübler-Ross, E. (2005) *On grief and grieving: Finding the meaning of grief through the five stages of loss.* New York: Simon & Schuster.

> *Danny was in the middle of a high-conflict divorce. Each day he and his soon-to-be ex-wife traded multiple nasty emails blaming each other for everything under the sun. I convinced Danny to try one email using the Other/Context/Self formula to ask for what he wanted going forward. Skeptical, he agreed and together we composed a carefully-worded, congruent response to her most recent blaming accusation. Instead of the typical immediate slew of curses and blame he usually received as her response, she answered his questions in a measured and unemotional way. She even wrote that she appreciated his attempt to understand her feelings. Danny couldn't believe her response, and immediately began examining all his relationships for ways to be more congruent in his communications.*

Unless we are in a self- or other-destructive situation, we don't need to change our coping strategies overnight. Real change occurs as a process, as we practice and perfect new ways of achieving our goals. The success we experience reinforces us in continuing the new behaviors.

Every time we forget to be congruent or we slide back into a habitual behavior, we can embrace the opportunity to analyze why it happened and to better understand the nature of our old wounds, sensitivities and triggers. Consider these times a gift; they provide us with the opportunity to better understand the how and why of our unconscious reactions. Without these insights it is much more difficult to make unconscious behavior conscious.

Recall the Change Process Cycle in Chapter 1. Lasting change requires going through each phase of the cycle—practicing new skills until they become the new status quo. Acting congruently may be the single most rewarding communication skill we can apply. For this reason alone, it is satisfying to perfect and enjoy the positive outcome of watching relationships improve and grow.

Worksheet for Chapter 14: Behavior, Coping Stances & Defenses Example

Activity: Make up a situation and a response for each of the five Coping Stances.
Example Situation: *Tom & Joan want to go to a movie. Joan wants to see "Women in Love," and her husband, Tom, wants to see "Die Hard II."*

The Placating Stance Only Considers *Other*

> Tom: *"Joan, I'd like to see Die Hard II tonight."*
> Placating Joan: *"Okaayyy."*

The Blaming Stance Only Considers *Self*

> Tom: *"Joan, I'd like to see Die Hard II tonight."*
> Blaming Joan: *"You are so inconsiderate. You don't even care that I want to see Women in Love tonight. It's my movie or forget it."*

The Super-Reasonable (Computer) Stance Only Considers *Context* or Facts

> Tom: *"Joan, I'd like to see Die Hard II tonight."*
> Computer Joan: *"Well, I'd like to see Women in Love, so we should find a third movie that starts at the right time."*

The Irrelevant (Distractor) & Stonewalling Stance: Avoids *Other, Context* and *Self*

> Tom: *"Joan, I'd like to see Die Hard II tonight."*
> Distracting Joan: *"Did you like what I cooked for dinner tonight?"*

The Congruent Coping Stance Incorporates the *Self*, the *Other*, and the *Context*

> **The Congruent Coping Stance Formula**
> 1) Acknowledge what the Other person might be thinking, wanting, needing.
> 2) What does the situation require?
> 3) What specific outcome would I like?

> 1) "Tom, I know that you would like to see Die Hard II tonight.
> 2) We both need a nice evening out together to relax and enjoy each other.
> 3) I'd really like to see Women in Love, but I'd be willing to see your movie tonight if we could see mine tomorrow night, or vice versa."

Chapter 14 Worksheet: Behavior, Coping Stances & Defenses

Activity: Make up a situation with a response for each of the five Coping Stances.
Situation: _____

_____

The Placating Stance Only Considers *Other*

_____
_____
_____

The Blaming Stance Only Considers *Self*

_____
_____
_____

The Super-Reasonable (Computer) Stance Only Considers *Context* **or Facts**

_____
_____
_____

The Irrelevant (Distractor), Stonewalling Stance: Avoids *Other, Context* **and** *Self*

_____
_____
_____

Congruent Response:

> **The Congruent Coping Stance Formula**
> **Incorporates the** *Other*, **the** *Context* **and the** *Self*
> 1) Acknowledge what the Other person might be thinking, wanting, needing.
> 2) What does the situation require?
> 3) What specific outcome would I like?

1) _____

2) _____

3) _____

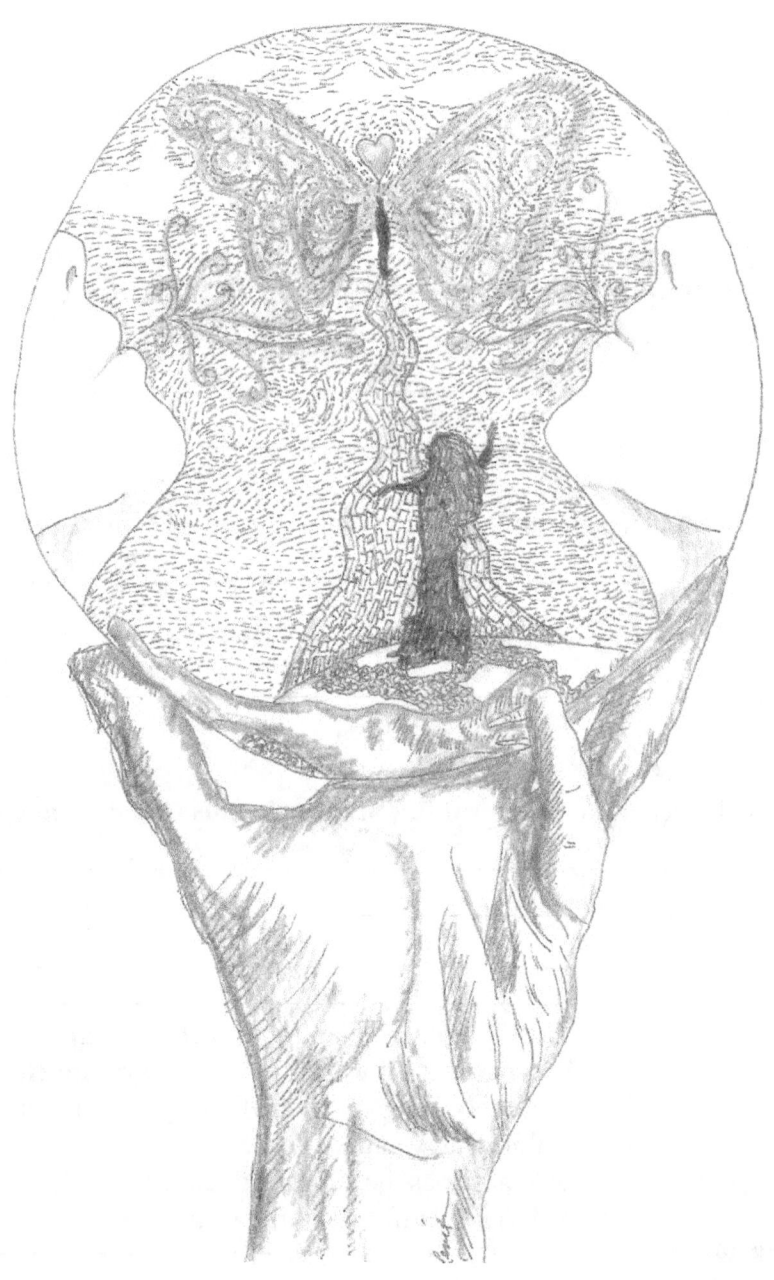

Chapter Fifteen: Conclusion, Hopes & Wishes

"We can learn something new anytime we believe we can." —Virginia Satir

As I pondered what I might write to conclude this collection of practical and philosophical life strategies, I retraced my steps toward the conception, gestation, labor and delivery of this "baby." I recalled my experiences in my family of origin: passing through developmental stages, overcoming challenges, and applying strategies that either worked or taught me valuable life lessons. I re-cherished memories of being married, raising children, nurturing friendships, resolving conflicts, recovering from the loss, hurt or fear that injected painful detours along the way. My goal was always to know and fulfill my purpose in life—my contribution to healing the world, helping myself and others find their own peace within and between.

I have found it very helpful to think about change as new ways of being more fully myself. When we look at embracing new possibilities as a means of achieving wholeness and fulfillment, we are more willing to begin the journey to self and other awareness; one that opens options for greater joy in life.

Peace Within, Peace Between focuses on many facets of self-improvement. Getting to know ourselves involves many things—not just retracing history but trying to understand why we created our personal stories the way we did. Human behavior is only the tip of the iceberg. Beneath that are our perceptions, our feelings and feelings about our feelings, our expectations and yearnings. All inform our *sense of Self* and determine what drives us, and what potential gifts we bring to the world.

This book presents some of Virginia Satir's work with its evolving practical application to life experience, as I have come to use it. It is focused on supporting you, personally or professionally, in achieving a vibrant relationship to yourself and others, i.e. Peace Within, Peace Between.

In the tradition of the Conclusion also acting as a review of the journey traveled, below is a summary of key ideas to help cement the insights and skills you've collected along the way.

Key Elements Review

In *Part One: Bugs with Solutions,* we began with the basic motivation for change (crisis and process) and the immediate resources, tools and insight we can apply to achieve positive change.

In *Part Two: New Information*, we continue to develop new perspectives for achieving personal and interpersonal goals. This section addresses what it means to be openly connected to Self and others; how to make and improve contact using more effective conversation techniques; finding positive intention to allow growth, healing of old wounds, living with integrity and risking true intimacy.

Part Three: Getting To Know Your Self develops the psychological cornerstones of self-awareness. It offers frameworks for identifying our personal characteristics: Learning Style—an inherent quality of our perception of life that we need to understand and appreciate; Personality Type—using the Myers-Briggs typology to reframe conflict as misunderstanding based on expectations and perspective; Core Values—staying congruent and consistent, defusing disproportionate reactions through the clues they provide about our deeper values and experiences; Assessment—to understand and optimize the qualities that make us unique and allow us to see the whole picture of our gifts, challenges and potential.

Part Four: Old Business, New Possibilities tackles the substantial challenge of getting from who we are now, to who we could be. Family of Origin (FOO) rules are explored in greater depth; these often faulty principles are reframed to open us to new possibilities for the future. Here family moves to the full spotlight with Satir's introduction of Family Therapy—creating a safe therapeutic environment exploring family roles with her approaches using Family Sculpting, stories and illustrations. Communication, the central pillar of Satir Family Therapy, is deconstructed for easy access; acronyms such as TAR and OCS describe how we can craft effective congruent communication. And when we fail, the power of the OCS approach continues in the effective apology.

Finally Satir's iceberg model for human behavior surfaces again (last seen in chapter 8), this time to spotlight coping stances—primal behaviors that resurface when we feel anxious or defensive. Again the functional value of OCS is reinforced using the congruent coping stance, and to recognize dysfunctional coping stances (Placating, Blaming, Distractor, Computer and Stonewalling). When we become conscious of the deficiencies in our communications, we can add the missing elements of OCS to move from being trapped in the past to a brighter, more congruent and authentic future.

Hopes

Life is always going to present us with both challenges and gifts; sometimes they come in the same package. Change will occur with or without our approval or readiness; we can resist it or work to learn from it. The longer we live, the more these changes can affect our mobility, well-being and life choices. Pain is inevitable, suffering optional. Achieving inner peace, regardless of what is happening around us requires staying present, maintaining consciousness and the resolve to stay in integrity—even when we don't understand why something is happening to us (or our loved ones). It is at these times a community, a family, friends and spiritual beliefs are mobilized to provide hope and support; the times that our success at building connection, nurturing and maintaining peace between us and others lightens our journey.

Because we aren't given a map for living life, there is no way to avoid the detours and bottlenecks that slow us. However, sometimes detours are beautiful and valuable; we wouldn't want to have missed them. My hope is that this book will act as a map to help you decide which path to take when you reach a fork in the road, how to grow from the detours, and even how to find different routes to reach your destinations. Life forces us to make thousands of choices every step of the way. I hope the ideas and skills you've learned and practiced here will be your emotional GPS, suggesting new routes to help you reach your destination, making the most of those obstacles and detours.

Each of us is a complex combination of our personal qualities and our environmental influences. As we learn more about our mind-body connections, how intimately all the parts of our body and mind are inter-connected, it has become a truism that we can't afford to have negative thoughts and emotions driving our behavior. If what we say and do are just the tip of the iceberg, then conscious management of our emotions in more positive directions is critically important. When we know, accept, and learn from our feelings, we grow stronger, healthier relationships with ourselves and others. We can change any less-than-positive feeling to a better one if we find the power to choose. My hope is that this book will help you claim that power going forward, connecting heart to heart, as well as mind to mind, in all your relationships and interactions.

Wishes

My sincere wish is that this book will provide the tools and inspiration you need to create the life you most desire—filled with purpose, passion and healthy, fulfilling relationships.

"The past is useful. It is the canvas upon which we paint our future. It is not, however, a painting until we apply the paint."
  – Linda Powers Leviton

References and Resources Bibliography

In addition to the references cited here, this bibliography also includes works that have significantly shaped my practice. You may find them useful for further reading.

Adams, F. (1891). *The genuine works of Hippocrates.* New York, NY: William Wood.

American Psychiatric Association. (2013). *Diagnostic and statistical manual of mental disorders* (5th ed.). Washington, DC: Author.

Andreas, S. (1999). *Virginia Satir: The patterns of her magic.* Moab, UT: Real People Press. (previously published 1991, Palo Alto: Science & Behavior Books)

Bandler, R., & Grinder, J. (1979). *Frogs into princes.* Moab, UT; Real People Press.

Bandler, R., Grinder, J., & Satir, V. (1976). *Changing with families.* Palo Alto, CA: Science & Behavior Books.

Bouchard, T. J., Jr., Lykken, D. T., McGue, M., Segal, N. J., & Tellegen, A. (1990). Sources of human psychological differences: The Minnesota study of twins reared apart. *Science, v.250, n.4978, pp.* 223-228.

Brizendine, L. (2006). *The female brain.* New York, NY: Morgan Road Books.

Buscaglia, L. (1978). *Personhood: The art of being fully human.* Thorofare, NJ: Slack.

Cherokee tale of two wolves. Retrieved September 10, 2012 from http://wizdompath.wordpress.com/?s=cherokee

Dabrowski, K. (1964). *Positive disintegration.* Boston, MA: Little Brown.

Dabrowski, K. (1967). *Personality shaping through positive disintegration.* Boston, MA: Little Brown.

Dabrowski, K. (with Kawczak, A., & Piechowski, M. M.) (1970). *Mental growth through positive disintegration.* London: Gryf.

Forbes 400 richest people in America. Retrieved August 18, 2011, from www.forbes.com/forbes-400

Gardner, H. (2006). *Multiple intelligences: New horizons.* New York, NY: Basic Books.

Gunderson, J., & Berkowitz, C. (2006). *A BPD Brief.* White Plains, NY: Borderline Personality Disorder Center.

Hendrix, H. (1988). *Getting the love you want: A guide for couples.* New York, NY: Pocket Books.

Jainworld Global Resource Center. (2012). *Elephant and the blind men.* Retrieved September 11, 2012 from www.jainworld.com/education/stories25.asp

Jones, W.H. S. (1923). *General introduction to Hippocrates* (Vol. 1). Cambridge, MA: Harvard University Press.

Jung, C. G. (1971). *Psychological types* (H. G. Baynes, trans.) *Collected works of C. G. Jung* (Vol. 6). Princeton, NJ: Princeton University Press. (Original work published 1923)

Keirsey, D., & Bates, M. (1978). *Please understand me: Character and temperament types.* Del Mar, CA: Prometheus Nemesis Books.

Kramer, S. Z. (1995). *Transforming the inner and outer family.* Binghamton, NY: Haworth Press.

Kübler-Ross, E. (2005). *On grief and grieving: Find the meaning of grief through the five stages of loss.* New York, NY: Simon & Schuster.

Leary, T. (1957). *Interpersonal diagnosis of personality: A functional theory and methodology.* New York, NY: John Wiley & Sons.

Leahy, M. M. (2004). *1001 questions to ask before you get married.* Columbus, OH: McGraw-Hill.

Leviton, L. P. (2011, May). Some characteristics of a tactile-kinesthetic learner; Gotta dance. *Gifted Development Newsletter*, pp. 1-3. [Available from communications@gifteddevelopment.com].

Myers, I. B. (1962). *Manual: The Myers-Briggs Type Indicator.* Palo Alto, CA: Consulting Psychologists Press.

Myers, I. B. (with P. B. Myers). (1980). *Gifts differing.* Palo Alto, CA: Consulting Psychologists Press.

Myers, I. B., & McCaulley, M. H. (1985). *Manual: A guide to the development and use of the Myers-Briggs Type Indicator.* Palo Alto, CA: Consulting Psychologists Press.

Nerin, W. (1995). *Family reconstruction: Long day's journey into light.* New York, NY: W. W. Norton.

Pavlina, S. *List of values.* Retrieved December 10, 2011, from www.stevepavlina.com/articles/list-of-values.htm

Powell, R. R. (2003). *History of personality theory.* Retrieved December 15, 2011, from www.armchair_academic.homestead.com/HistoryPer.html

Right brain vs. left brain test: Optical illusion. Retrieved December 11, 2011, from www.youtube.com/watch?v=9CEr2GfGilw

Rokeach, M. (1973). *The nature of human values.* New York, NY: The Free Press.

Rudacille, D. *Diagnostic tests for autism may miss many girls.* Retrieved December 13, 2011, from sfari.org/news-and-opinion/news/2011/diagnostic-tests-for-autism-may-miss-many-girls

Satir, V. (1964). *Conjoint family therapy.* Palo Alto, CA: Science & Behavior Books.

Satir, V. (1972). *Peoplemaking.* Palo Alto, CA: Science & Behavior Books.

Satir, V. (1975). *Self-esteem.* Millbrae, CA: Celestial Arts.

Satir, V. (1976). *Making contact.* Millbrae, CA: Celestial Arts.

Satir, V. (1978). *Your many faces.* Millbrae, CA: Celestial Arts.

Satir, V. (1988). *The new peoplemaking.* Palo Alto, CA: Science & Behavior Books.

Satir, V., & Baldwin, M. (1983). *Satir Step by Step.* Palo Alto, CA: Science & Behavior Books.

Satir, V., Banmen, J., Gerber, J., & Gomori, M. (1991). *The Satir model: Family therapy and beyond.* Palo Alto, CA: Science & Behavior Books.

Satir, V., Stachowiak, J., & Tachman, H. A. (1994). *Helping families to change.* Palo Alto, CA: Science & Behavior Books.

Schwab, J., Baldwin, M., Geber, J., Gomori, M. & Satir, V. (1989). *The Satir approach to communication: A workshop manual.* Palo Alto, CA: Science & Behavior Books.

Virginia Satir, Journals (Unpublished, undated personal correspondence with Nancy MacDonald).

Silverman, L. K. (2002). *Upside-down brilliance: The visual-spatial learner.* Denver, CO: DeLeon.

Silverstein, S. (1982). *The missing piece meets the big O.* New York, NY: Harper & Row.

Wegscheider-Cruse, S. (1994). *Family reconstruction.* Palo Alto, CA: Science & Behavior Books.

Wright, L. (1998). *Twins and what they tell us about who we are.* New York, NY: John Wiley & Sons.

Index

—A—

acceptance 187
Annemarie Roeper 125
apology 173
appreciations 145
appropriateness 159, 161, 169
AS .... See: Asperger Syndrome
Asperger Syndrome 48, 49, 71
assessment 123, 124, 125, 129
asynchronous development 24, 123, 126
auditory-sequential 84, 85, 86, 167
autism 48, 126, 136
Autism Spectrum 48
Avanta iii

—B—

Bank Accounts. .... See: Emotional Bank Accounts
behavior 95, 96, 97, 98, 115, 175
belief ... 58, 60, 65, 70, 137, 139, 144, 147, 148
blame 10, 35, 57, 58, 59, 148, 168, 188
blaming 58, 106, 145, 180, 184, 188
Blaming Coping Stance 180
Bob and Becky Spitzer iii
Borderline Personality Disorder 9, 75
Bugs with Solutions 1

—C—

Carl Jung 96, 125
Change Process 5, 6
chaos 5
communication ... 5, 11, 20, 31, 41, 47, 48, 49, 52, 86, 87, 111, 124, 143, 145, 159, 160, 161, 163, 164, 165, 166, 167, 170, 173, 178, 179, 183, 184, 188

compassion 5, 76, 96, 116, 126, 145, 153, 164, 178, 181
Computer Coping Stance .... See: Super-reasonable Coping Stance
congruent... 11, 12, 18, 53, 150, 160, 177, 178, 179, 184, 188, 191
Congruent Coping Stance 178
context 7, 22, 52, 53, 58, 70, 100, 104, 111, 116, 117, 124, 138, 143, 147, 149, 150, 159, 160, 165, 166, 171, 173, 178, 180, 181, 189, 191
coping stances 175, 177, 189
core values ... 17, 109, 110, 111, 112, 113, 114, 115, 116, 117, 118, 119, 121
Couples Therapy 119
creative 3, 87, 88, 93, 126, 131, 178

—D—

defense mechanisms 64, 150, 185, 186, 187
defenses 175
denial defense 186
differentiation 47
discussion script 171
displaced hurt 62
Dissociative Identity Disorder 186
Distractor .... See: Irrelevant Coping Stance
dysfunctional behaviors 58
dysfunctional coping stances 179

—E—

EBA .... See: Emotional Bank Accounts
Elizabeth Seward iv
Emotional Bank Accounts 50, 52, 55

Emotional Banking System 50
empathy 5, 20, 40, 116, 126, 153
ethics 75
exceptionalities 3
extroversion 100, 107

—F—

Failure to Thrive Syndrome 5
family map 24, 25, 145
Family of Origin 57, 65
Family Reconstruction 59
Family Sculpting 151
Family Therapy 143, 144
FOO .... See: Family of Origin

—G—

genogram 24, 145
gifted .... vii, 3, 21, 22, 24, 33, 88, 123
good will units 50
good will values 55
guilt 13, 17, 39, 45, 115, 153, 179, 187

—H—

Harville Hendrix 119
hemispheric preference 83, 84, 85
hierarchical 17, 18, 86
Hippocrates 98
homeschool 126
Houston 87
Humoralism 98

—I—

iceberg 95, 175
ignoring defense 186
IHLRN- International Human Learning Resource Network iii

Imago Therapy 119
incongruent 11
insight 24, 34, 37, 39, 65, 66, 100, 129, 135, 137, 150, 161
integrity 109, 112, 115, 117, 119, 121, 137, 150, 152
intimacy 69, 76, 79
introversion 100, 107
Introversion-Extroversion 100
intuitive 102
Irrelevant Coping Stance 182, 183, 189, 191
Isabelle Briggs Myers 99

—J—

Jean Houston 87
Jean Piaget 125
judging 104, 107
Judging-Perceiving 104
Jung 96

—K—

Katharine Cook Briggs 99
Kazimierz Dabrowski 125
Kiersey Temperament Sorter 100

—L—

Larry Seward iv
learning disabilities 123, 124
learning styles 3, 83, 84, 88, 89, 90, 92, 167
Linda Silverman .... iii, 21, 89, 125

—M—

Maria Montessori 125
mariposas iii
Martin Buber 125
MBTI 99

meanings.... 12, 34, 52, 61, 83, 87, 95, 96, 135, 139, 167, 175

mentors .... iii, 19, 21, 22, 29, 71

multi-generational transmission process 57

Myers-Briggs Personality Type Inventory ... 24

Myers-Briggs Type Indicator 96, 99

—N—

Nancy Macdonald iii

Neurolinguistic Programming 10, 115

—O—

OCS .... See: Other Context Self

other... 164, 171, 173, 178, 179, 180, 183, 189, 191

Other Context Self 49, 159, 160, 164, 168, 169, 171, 173, 178, 182, 188, 189

—P—

passive-aggressive 179

perceiving 104, 107

perception 10, 13, 33, 39, 52, 86, 143, 148, 149, 153

personality disorder 75

personality type 24, 96, 97, 98, 99, 106, 107

Placating Coping Stance 179

positive change 10

positive connection with a therapist 39

positive connections in the world 40

positive intention 60

primary triad 19

projection 187

—Q—

qualitative assessments 124

—R—

relationships... vii, 5, 10, 18, 20, 33, 36, 37, 38, 45, 59, 60, 63, 72, 73, 74, 75, 76, 77, 87, 96, 97, 98, 107, 109, 115, 118, 119, 135, 136, 143, 144, 146, 151, 169, 177, 179, 181, 182, 184, 185, 187, 188

relevance 159, 163, 169

role models 21

Ron Nelson iii

—S—

Satir Family Camp .... iii, 20, 117

Satir Global Network iii

self 166, 171, 173, 178, 180, 183, 189, 191

sensing 102, 107

Sensing-Intuitive 102

Shel Silverstein 8

status quo 7, 151, 188

Steve Pavlina 112

Stonewalling Coping Stance 183, 189, 191

Super-reasonable Coping Stance 181

—T—

tactile-kinesthetic 84, 85, 86, 88, 167

Tale of Two Wolves 153

TAR .. See: Timing Appropriateness Relevance

The Beautiful People iii

The Missing Piece Meets the Big O 8

Thinking-Feeling 103

Tikkun Olam viii

timing 159, 160, 169

Timing Appropriateness Relevance 159

Timothy Leary 9

transformation 3, 7, 17, 143, 144, 149

trust 5, 17, 18, 21, 24, 27, 33, 39, 40, 46, 70, 74, 102, 135, 137, 150, 159, 162, 186

—U—

Unfairness Reflex.................................... 62, 63

—V—

values.........19, 22, 52, 57, 65, 71, 75, 112, 113, 115, 119, 137, 147, 151, 152, 181

violence................................12, 13, 62, 73, 185

Virginia Satir. iii, v, vi, 1, 3, 17, 24, 31, 33, 42, 45, 57, 69, 81, 83, 95, 109, 117, 123, 125, 133, 135, 143, 159, 175, 177

visual-spatial..................84, 85, 86, 87, 89, 167

—W—

Whole Child Assessment
    WCA 124, 125, 126

wisdom.......................................18, 22, 26, 181

About the Author

Linda Powers Leviton, M.A., is a licensed Marriage, Family and Child Therapist who counsels, coaches and consults people of all ages on a range of topics related to communication, relationships, parenting, education, giftedness and learning styles. She currently is the West Coast Director of the Gifted Development Center (www.gifteddevelopment.com).

Linda grew up in Los Angeles, Ca. with two handicapped siblings, attending GATE programs in LAUSD. She met Dr. Linda Silverman in 1964. This led to a life-long mentorship, friendship, and professional collaboration including co-authoring articles such as "In Search of the Perfect Program," which has been reprinted six times and continues to be relevant more than 20 years after its first publication.

Graduating from Pitzer College with honors in Psychology and Art, she attended the Claremont Graduate School Teaching Internship Program and eventually Phillips Graduate Institute in Clinical Counseling. Since 1974, Ms. Leviton has developed and taught programs to help parents and educators best reach children with learning and emotional challenges, particularly the twice exceptional, those who are gifted and also challenged with social, emotional or learning challenges.

Ms. Leviton offers training programs and workshops to help teachers, parents and administrators identify and teach visual-spatial and gifted learners (www.visualspatial.org) and she has written numerous articles on learning style, giftedness and personality. Other avocations include art, cartooning, being married for 25 years and raising three gifted and creative children. She can be reached at:
www.leviton.org or www.giftedandcreativecounseling.com or by e-mail: linda@leviton.org

Forward Author

Linda Kreger Silverman, Ph.D., is a licensed psychologist. She founded the Institute for the Study of Advanced Development, and its subsidiaries, Gifted Development Center (GDC) and Visual-Spatial Resource in Denver, Colorado. In the last 33 years, she has studied 6,000 children who have been assessed at GDC, the largest data bank on this population. This research enabled the creation of extended norms on the WISC-IV and WPPSI-IV. Her Ph.D. is in educational psychology and special education from the University of Southern California. For nine years, she served on the faculty of the University of Denver in counseling psychology and gifted education. She has been studying the psychology and education of the gifted since 1961 and has written over 300 articles, chapters and books, including Counseling the Gifted and Talented, Upside-Down Brilliance: The Visual-Spatial Learner and Advanced Development: A Collection of Works on Gifted Adults. Her latest book, Giftedness 101, was released early in 2013 (New York: Springer).
Websites: www.gifteddevelopment.com and www.visualspatial.org

SCIENCE AND BEHAVIOR BOOKS, INC.
Publishing books about counseling, psychology, family therapy, and recovery. Main publisher of and about Virginia Satir.

Other Titles:

- *Another Chance: Hope & Health for the Alcoholic Family,* Sharon Wegscheider-Cruse
- *Conjoint Family Therapy, third edition,* Virginia Satir
- *The Creative Connection, Expressive Arts as Healing,* Natalie Rogers
- *The Creative Connection for Groups, Person-Centered Expressive Arts as Healing and Social Change,* Natalie Rogers
- *Experiential Therapy for Co-Dependency,* Sharon Wegscheider-Cruse, Joseph Cruze, George Bougher
- *Family Reconstruction; The Living Theater Model,* Sharon Wegscheider-Cruse, Kathy Higby, Ted Klontz, Ann Rainey
- *The Gestalt Approach & Eye Witness to Therapy,* Fritz Perls
- *Grandparenting,* Sharon Wegscheider-Cruse
- *I'd Give My Life! A Journey by Folk Music,* Erik Darling
- *Integrated Treatment of Child Sexual Abuse,* Henry Giarretto
- *Into the Dark for Gold,* Les Rhodes
- *The New Peoplemaking,* Virginia Satir
- *Passion For Freedom – Maria's Story,* Maria Gomori
- *Peer Counseling, Skills, Ethics and Perspectives,* edited by Vincent J. D'Andrea and Peter Salovey
- *Positive Regard, Carl Rogers & Other Notables He Influenced,* Melvin H. Suhd, Ed.
- *A Resource Handbook for Satir Concepts,* compiled by Johanna Schwab
- *The Satir Approach to Communication: a Workshop Manual,* Johanna Schwab, Michele Baldwin, Jane Gerber, Maria Gomori, Virginia Satir
- *Satir Family Camp: An Intentional Community,* Elsa Ten Broeck and Mary D. Garrison
- *The Satir Model: Family Therapy and Beyond,* John Banmen, Jane Gerber, Maria Gomori
- *Satir Step by Step, a Guide to Creating Change in Families,* Michele Baldwin
- *SATIR Transformational Systemic Therapy,* edited by John Banmen
- *The Skipping Stone: Ripple Effects of Mental Illness on the Family,* second edition, Mona Wasow
- *The Structure of Magic, Vol. I & II,* Richard Bandler and John Grinder
- *The Viola in My Life, An Alto Rhapsody,* Bernard Zaslav
- *Virginia Satir: Her Life & Circle of Influence,* Melvin M. Suhd, Laura Dodson, and Maria Gomori
- *Walking on Water: Self-Esteem and a Journey of Faith,* Robert Ball